Inmate Journal

ISBN 9798447072247

This publication is designed to provide accurate and authoritative information in regard to the subject matter covered. It is sold with the understanding that neither the author nor the publisher is engaged in rendering legal, investment, accounting or other professional services. While the publisher and author have used their best efforts in preparing this book, they make no representations or warranties with respect to the accuracy or completeness of the contents of this book and specifically disclaim any implied warranties of merchantability or fitness for a particular purpose. No warranty may be created or extended by sales representatives or written sales materials. The advice and strategies contained herein may not be suitable for your situation. You should consult with a professional when appropriate. Neither the publisher nor the author shall be liable for any loss of profit or any other commercial damages, including but not limited to special, incidental, consequential, personal, or other damages.

Book Cover by Patricia Branigan
Illustrations by Patricia Branigan
1st edition 2022
2nd edition 2024
For bulk order please contact
butterybraniganbooks@gmail.com
or visit www.butterybraniganbooks.com

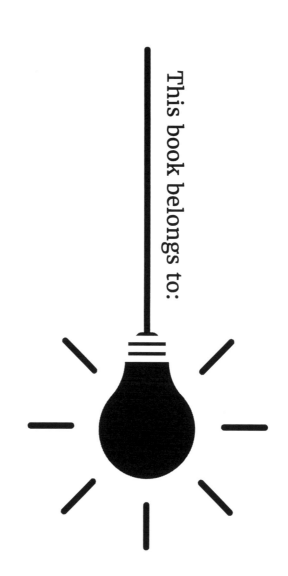

This book belongs to:

Affirmations

I am stronger than my circumstances.

Each day, I am growing and evolving.

My past does not define my future.

I am worthy of love, respect, and kindness.

I choose to focus on what I can control today.

I am learning from my mistakes and becoming a better person.

I have the power to create a positive future.

My mind is free, even if my body is not.

I am capable of change and transformation.

I am finding peace within myself, no matter where I am.

My strength lies in how I rise after I fall.

I choose to release shame and embrace self-compassion.

I am not alone; I have people who care about me.

I can still make a meaningful impact on the world.

Every challenge I face makes me stronger.

I am in charge of my thoughts, and I choose positivity.

My life still holds purpose and meaning.

I forgive myself for past mistakes and allow myself to move forward.

My Affirmations

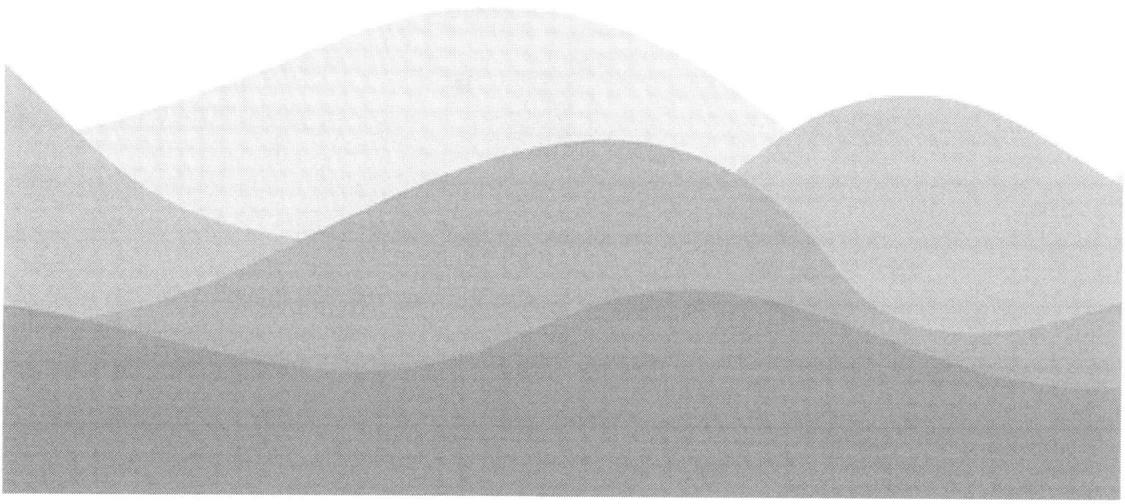

My Affirmations

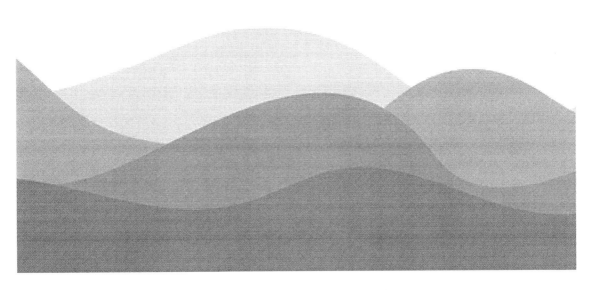

The Power of 1%
Transform Your Life with Small Changes

A Simple Path to Misery:
Want your life to be different → Could make a change → Won't make that change → Be miserable.

A Path to Transformation:
Want your life to be different → Could make a change → Will make a change → Joyful transformation.

You don't have to make the changes all at once. Start small. Even one percent changes will add up over time. Maybe you can change what you focus on and be one percent more positive. You could practice meditation and be one percent more mindful. You could seek joy and be one percent happier. You do have the ability to change your life for the better.

Start by taking a look at your daily routines and habits. Write down everything you do regularly, from when you wake up to when you go to bed. Once you have your list, think about how you can adjust these habits to get closer to your goals. Small changes can add up over time.

As you think about your daily routines, consider making small changes that can make a difference, even in your current situation. You could use some time each day to connect with others, like sending one of the cards in this book to someone you care about. You could take care of your body by exercising or choosing healthier foods. You could also spend time reading or working toward your education goals each day.

These small changes might not seem like much on their own, but they can improve how you feel over time. By making these adjustments, you can slowly build a life that fits better with your values, even in prison. Every positive step you take adds up and gets you closer to the future you want.

Use a habit tracker as a visual of all the work you are doing.

Habit Tracker

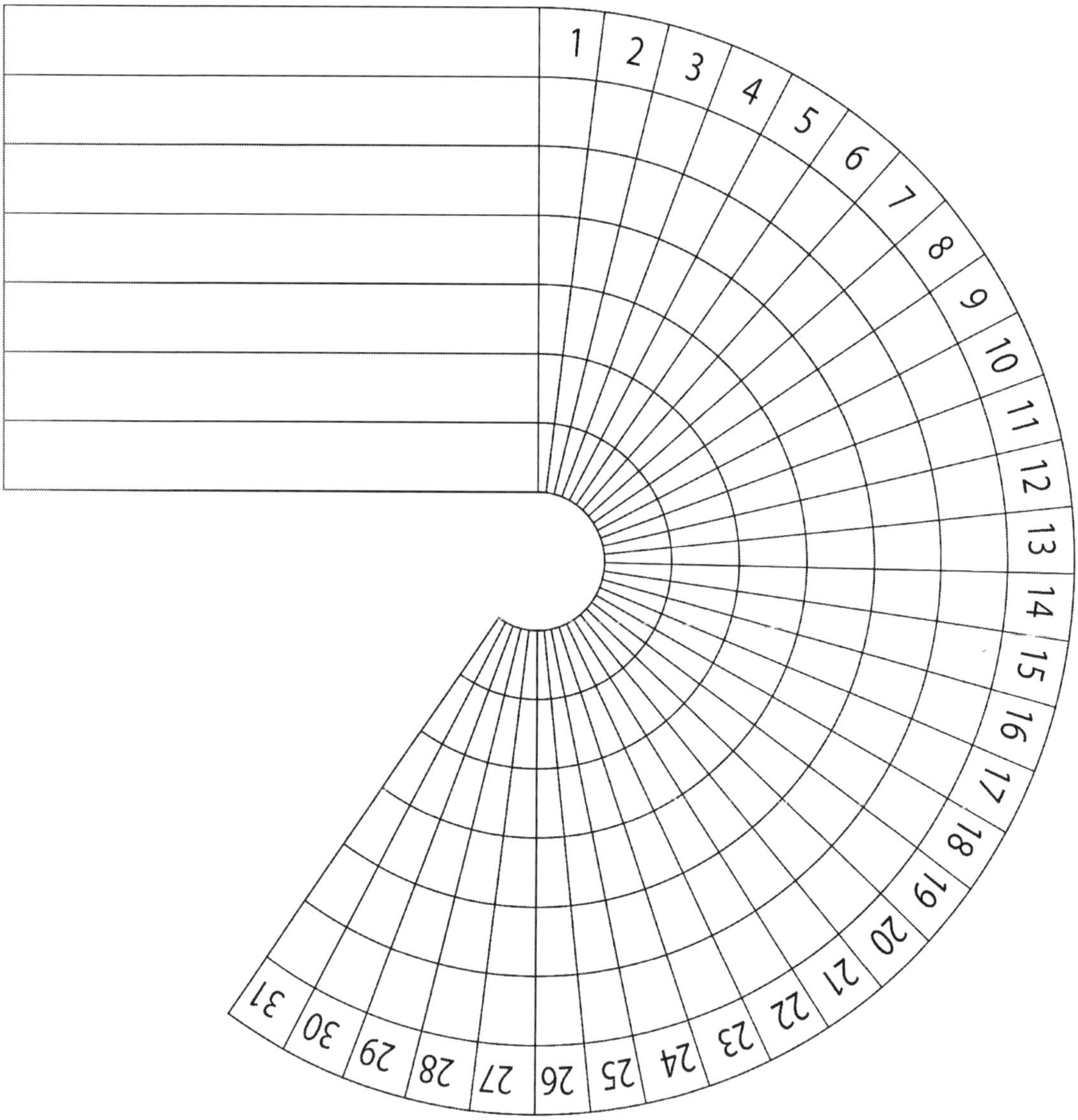

Make a list of the habits you want to work on.
For each day you accomplish a habit, color in the corresponding square.
If you don't accomplish the habit, leave the square blank.

This will create a visual representation of your efforts towards achieving the life you desire.

Habit Tracker

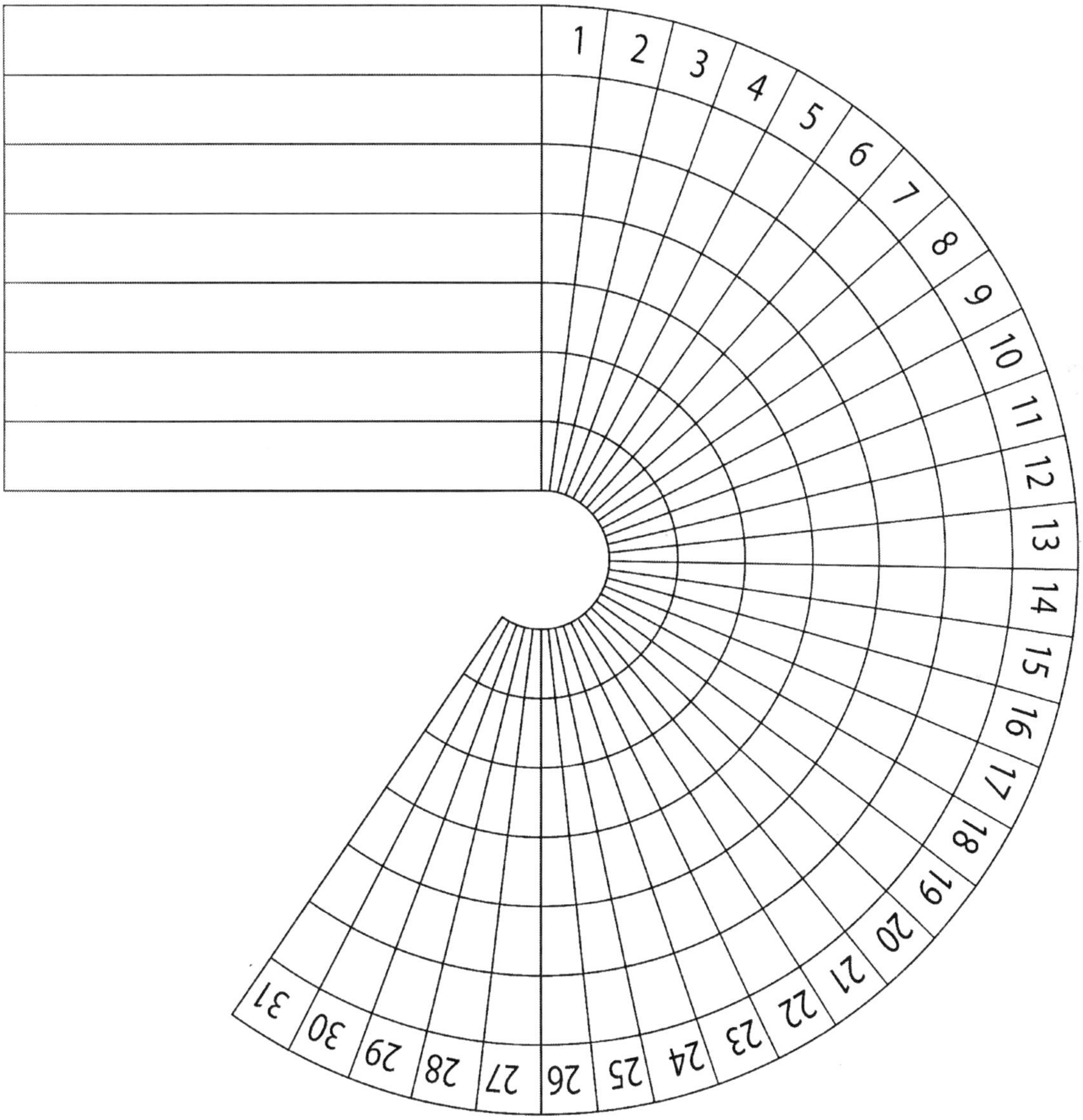

You can't control the wind
But you can adjust your sails

Focus On What You Can Control

In 1932, American theologian Reinhold Niebuhr wrote the Serenity Prayer. It goes like this:

"God, grant me the serenity to accept the things I cannot change, courage to change the things I can, and wisdom to know the difference."

Almost one hundred years ago, Niebuhr advised his followers to look at what they could and could not control and know there was a difference. There is a reason this advice is still relevant today. Knowing what you can control is one key to finding peace.

You might think this idea is nonsense, and you have no control over anything in your life. But I want to challenge you to think about what you can control. Right now, you're reading this book—you could have tossed it aside and done something else with your time, but you chose to keep reading. You have the power to decide whether or not you finish any part of this book or make any changes in your life. That is something you control.

You can control whether you spend your days looking for joy or misery. I guarantee you that whichever one you choose to look for, you will find.

There are things in your life you have no control over, such as what other people do or say. But you do have control over your actions and how you will respond to situations that arise.

Your life may feel extremely challenging right now, and I don't want to downplay your struggle. But wouldn't you want to go for happiness if there's a chance for happiness? Knowing what you can control can help you find more peace and joy. Take a moment to think about what's in your hands and what isn't, and choose to move forward with a positive attitude.

"Make the best use of what is in your power, and take the rest as it happens."

- Epictetus

I can’t control, so I let go.

I focus on what I can control

Inside the circle write all the things you can control. In the space outside the cirle write the things that you have no control over.

Learn to Meditate

Meditation is important because it helps you slow down, clear your mind, and reduce stress. It's like giving your brain a break from all the noise and chaos of daily life. Sitting quietly and focusing on your breath can make you feel calmer, think more clearly, and improve your mood. It's a simple way to manage your mental health and feel more balanced in your everyday life.

Meditation can be challenging, and getting the hang of it takes time. It's called a "practice" because it really does take practice to learn how to calm your mind and body. Here are a few things to remember as you learn to meditate.

- Begin with just a few minutes each day. You can slowly increase your meditation time each week.
- Try to find a quiet spot. It doesn't have to be perfect; just try to find a place where noise is more minimal.
- You don't need to sit cross-legged on the floor unless you want to. Try sitting in a chair, on a cushion, or lying down. Choose what is most comfortable for you.
- There's no right or wrong way to meditate. If your mind drifts or you get distracted, that's okay. Just calmly bring your attention to your breath or whatever you're focusing on.
- Try to meditate at the same time each day. This helps build a routine and makes it easier to stick with it.
- Be patient with yourself—getting good at something starts with giving yourself a chance to try. It's better to try and not be perfect than never to try at all.
- Meditation can feel different each time. Some days will be easier than others, and that's normal.

Try out these different techniques and see what works best for you. Keep an open mind and see where it takes you.

Day One

- Pick an affirmation from the affirmation page or create your own.

- Sit in a comfortable position.

- Practice today's breathing exercise:
    - Take a deep breath, slowly filling your body with air—first your stomach, then your chest.
    - Breathe in deeply until you feel the breath in your throat.
    - Hold your breath for a count of two.
    - Slowly release all the air, starting with your throat, moving to your chest, and then your stomach.

- Repeat the breathing exercise five times.

- Repeat the affirmation in your mind or out loud a few times.

- Repeat the breathing exercise five times.

- Wrap your arms around yourself in a gentle hug.

Day Two

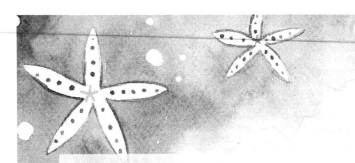

- Pick an affirmation from the affirmation page or create your own.
- Sit in a comfortable position.
- Stretch your arms over your head while taking a deep breath.
- As you breathe out, bring your arms down to rest on your legs, relaxing your arms and shoulders.
- Practice box breathing:
  - Breathe in for the count of four.
  - Hold for the count of four.
  - Breathe out for the count of four.
  - Hold for the count of four.
- Repeat four times.
- Try different counts up to ten.
- Say your affirmation three times in your mind.
- Practice box breathing four more times.
- Wrap your arms around yourself in a gentle hug.

Day Three

- Pick an affirmation from the affirmation page or create your own.
- Find a comfortable seated position.
- Place your hands on your knees.
- Take a deep breath through your nose and let the air out as quickly as possible, creating a haa sound in your mouth.
- Practice this three times, and then return your breath to normal.
- Imagine a single lit candle in your mind.
- Picture the flame as it dances and moves.
- Repeat your chosen positive affirmation in your mind. When thoughts come into your mind, acknowledge them without judgment. Picture them as clouds overhead, moving through and out of your mind. Bring your focus back to the flame.
- If you'd like to try something different, picture yourself sitting on a beach. Imagine the waves rolling in and out with the gentle breeze.
- Repeat your chosen positive affirmation in your mind. When other thoughts come into your mind, acknowledge them without judgment. Bring your thoughts back to the waves on the beach.
- When you feel calm and relaxed, take one more deep breath and quickly blow it out.
- Wrap your arms around yourself in a gentle hug.

Day Four

- Lay on your bed flat on your back.

- Mentally scan your body to identify any areas that feel tense.

- Begin with your feet.
    - How do your feet feel against your mattress?
    - Are any parts of your feet holding tension?

- Flex the muscles in your feet and then relax.

- Repeat a positive affirmation about your feet while taking a deep breath. For example, "My feet keep me grounded and help me move forward each day, and I'm thankful for their strength."

- Move to your legs.
    - How do your legs feel?
    - Are they relaxed or tense?
- Tense the muscles in your legs and then relax.

- Repeat a positive affirmation about your legs while taking a deep breath. For example, "I'm grateful for my legs and how they support me."

- Continue up the rest of your body. Tense and then relax one area at a time, repeating a positive affirmation for that body part.

- When you are finished, take three deep breaths while relaxing your entire body.

Day Five

This meditation is simple and great for those times when meditation feels challenging. It's an easy way to calm your mind without feeling overwhelmed. Just follow along and let yourself relax—no pressure, just a moment to breathe and let go of stress.

- Take a deep breath, slowly filling your stomach with air.
    - Count to one, and then slowly release your breath.

- Take a deep breath, slowly filling your stomach with air.
    - Count to two, and then slowly release your breath.

- Keep going with this slow, steady breathing until you reach the count of twenty.

- Next, try to count backward, starting at twenty working your way back down to one.

- Don't worry if you lose count—you can start over if you want to, or guess where you left off and start from there.

- When you are finished, wrap yourself in a gentle hug.

- Send kindness to yourself for your efforts.

Grounding Techniques

Grounding Exercises to Calm Your Mind

When you're feeling anxious or stressed in your current situation, grounding is a simple technique to help you get back on track. Grounding helps you take your mind off your worries and feel more calm. Here are three ways to ground yourself when your circumstances feel overwhelming.

- Grounding with Your Senses. Look around and notice:
  - Five things you can see (objects around you)
  - Four things you can touch (like the ground or your clothes)
  - Three things you can hear (sounds around you)
  - Two things you can smell (the air or something nearby)
  - One thing you can taste (if possible)

- Rainbow Grounding. Look for objects matching the following colors:
  - Red
  - Orange
  - Yellow
  - Green
  - Blue
  - Purple

- Feet on the Ground:
  - Sit down.
  - Place your feet flat on the floor.
  - Press them firmly into the ground.
  - Feel the connection to the floor and remind yourself that you are here, safe, and in control.
  - Take a deep breath, letting your stomach fill with air.
  - Hold for several seconds.
  - Slowly release the breath as you repeat the affirmation I am calm.
  - Repeat for several minutes.

Tapping

Think about the issue you want to focus on while doing this exercise. It could be a fear or any other issue you're dealing with. Try coming up with a simple phrase that recognizes the issue while also being kind to yourself. Something like, "Even though I have this [fear or problem], I still fully accept myself." Think about what you are struggling with at this exact moment to create your phrase.

Here are a few examples:

- "Even though I'm in prison, I still accept myself just as I am."
- "Even though I'm not at my ideal weight, I still care for and accept my body."
- "Even though I'm dealing with anxiety, I still value and respect my mind."
- "Even though I'm away from my family right now, I still appreciate and accept who I am."

The Tapping Sequence

You can use one or more fingertips to tap with a pressure that feels comfortable to you. Tap each point below seven times, starting from the top and moving down your body in this order. While you tap, repeat the phrase you created three times.

1. The sides of your hand below the pinky finger. Tap both hands.
2. The top of your head
3. Your eyebrow
4. The side of your eye
5. Under your eye
6. Under your nose
7. Your chin
8. Your collarbone (one hand's width below your neck)
9. The sides of your body where your hand would be if you hugged yourself.

Tapping your fingers on different areas of your body activates pressure points that help calm and balance your mind and body.

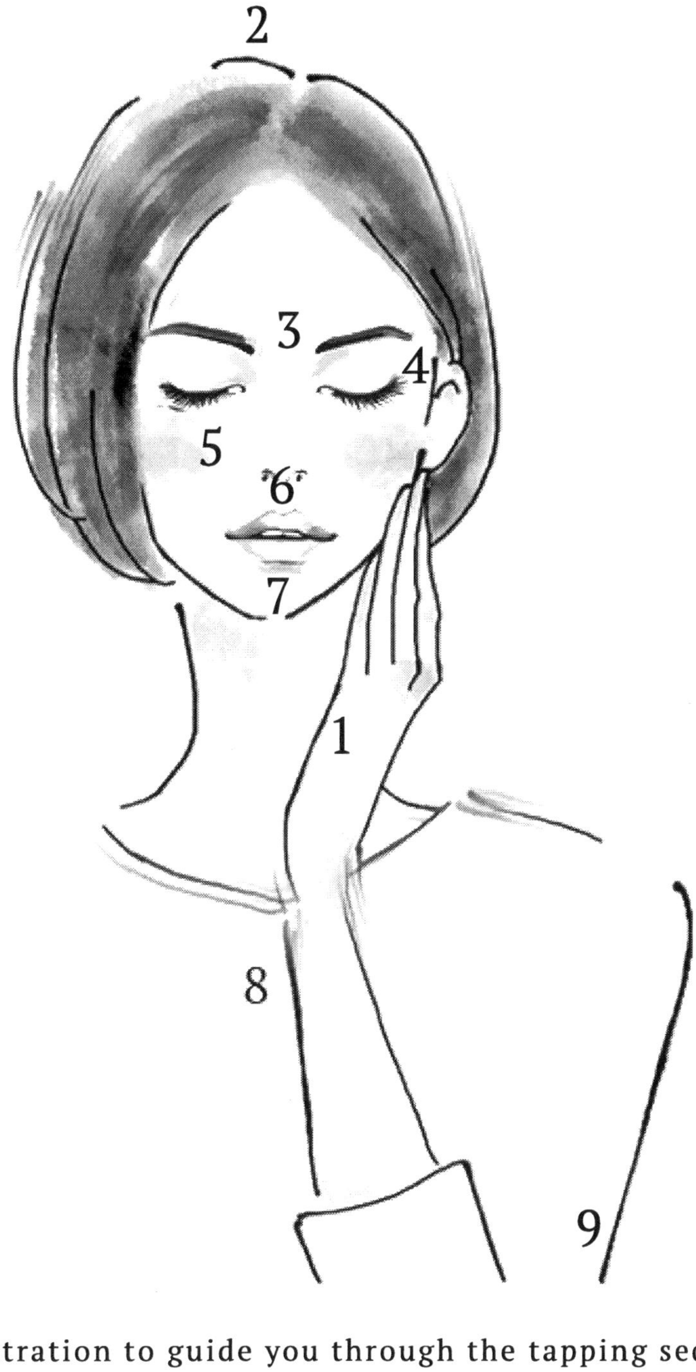

Use this illustration to guide you through the tapping sequence.

Mindful Thoughts: Journaling With or Without Paper

Journaling and thinking things over can be helpful as you start taking control of your life. Writing down or reflecting on your thoughts can give you a clearer picture of where you are and where you want to go. Here are some ways you can use journaling and reflecting while you're in prison:

- **Start a gratitude list:**
  - Gratitude can help you see your situation in a better light. When it's tough to find the positive, start with simple things you might overlook, like having food, shelter, or moments of peace.
  - Try to find small things you're thankful for each day, like a friendly conversation, a calm moment, or a kind act. Focusing on these things can help you notice more positives over time.
- **Face your frustrations:**
  - Imagine you're having a conversation about all the tough things in your life—your time in prison, mistakes from the past, or struggles with your mental health. In your mind or on paper, tell those things exactly how you feel without holding back.
  - This can help you understand that the challenging things you're going through don't define your worth. It's a way to release stuck emotions and get a clearer view.
- **Take a vacation in your mind:**
  - Picture a place you'd love to go—like a city, the countryside, the beach, or the mountains. Imagine the trip as if you're really there. Let your mind take a break from your current situation and enjoy this mental getaway. A short escape in your imagination can help you feel refreshed and ready to handle things better.
- **Seek joy and celebrate the good days:**
  - When you have a good day, write it down, share it with someone, or just take a moment to think about it. Keep a list of the happy moments in your life. These little bits of joy can help you through the tough times.
  - Remember, what you focus on is what you'll notice more of. By looking for the good, you'll see more of it. There are good moments out there—start paying attention, and you'll find them.
- **Seek the positive about yourself:**
  - Take time to think of all the good things about you! If it's hard to do, consider what a close friend or family member might say about you. Or even imagine what your pet would say if they could talk! It's important to remind yourself that you're valuable and to show yourself some kindness.
  - Write positive words that describe you in the thought bubbles.

A letter to you,

We want to recognize the hard work you are putting into your personal growth during this difficult time. The things you are going through require a lot of strength and determination. We encourage you to keep pushing forward—your efforts are meaningful and will make a difference.

What you're going through is hard and can feel like too much. But every little step you take to improve yourself and every small win counts. You're doing the work that will help you now and in the future.

Sometimes, it can feel like you're alone. You are not. We are here with you, rooting for you. You might feel like you are not doing enough, but we think you are. Every moment of patience, self-reflection, and effort to improve makes a difference. You're working on your future, even if it is a long and uncertain journey. Your dedication to yourself shows your commitment to growth.

Don't let the opinions of others weigh you down. Remember the words of Bernard Baruch: "Be who you are and say what you feel, because those who mind don't matter, and those who matter don't mind." Stand tall and be proud of the work you're doing to turn your life around.

It's also important to take care of yourself in this journey. Take time to rest and care for your mental health. You deserve peace and well-being as much as anyone else. Your resilience is something to be proud of, but it's also okay to lean on others for support when needed.

You're doing an amazing job; we admire your strength and determination. Please know that you're not alone in this—you have people standing by your side, cheering you on every step of the way.

With all our support,
Patricia and Beth

I
Seek Joy

I'm Grateful

Things I Love About Me

Opposite Action

Identify the Emotion: Start by recognizing the intense emotion you're experiencing. It could be anger, anxiety, sadness, or any other strong feeling.

Describe the Action You're Inclined to Take: What is your typical response or action when feeling this emotion? For instance, if you're feeling angry your typical response might be to punch a wall or scream.

Consider the Opposite Action: Now, think about what the opposite action would be. What would you do if you were feeling the complete opposite emotion? For example, if you are feeling angry and want to cause physical pain to yourself or someone else, the opposite might be to meditate and discover a peaceful emotion.

Try the Opposite Action: Challenge yourself to take the opposite action. Even if it feels uncomfortable, give it a try.

Notice the Effects: After taking the opposite action, pay close attention to how you feel. Did your emotional intensity decrease? Did your perspective shift?

This exercise can be helpful because it pushes you to try something new. It helps you break out of your usual reactions to emotions and gives you a chance to take control of how you respond.

Remember, the goal isn't to ignore your feelings but to deal with them in a way that helps you reach your long-term goals in the healthiest way possible.

"We cannot solve our problems with the same thinking we used when we created them." *-Albert Einstein*

Identify the emotion:

____

Your typical action when you are experiencing this emotion:

____

____

Write down an opposite action:

____

Notice any physical effects:

____

Notice any emotional effects:

____

Notice any social effects -how did this new action affect others:

____

Identify the emotion:

____

Your typical action when you are experiencing this emotion:

____

____

Write down an opposite action:

____

Notice any physical effects:

____

Notice any emotional effects:

____

Notice any social effects -how did this new action affect others:

____

Tips for Better Communication

"Never argue with a fool; onlookers may not be able to tell the difference."
— Mark Twain.

Emotions can run strong in prison. The environment can make people act in ways that push your buttons, bringing up intense emotions. These feelings are normal, but it can be hard to talk things through when everyone is upset. Here are some tips to help you communicate better in prison and on the outside:

- **Take a Moment to Deep Breath:**
  - Before starting any serious talk, take a moment to calm down. Being calm makes a big difference, whether you're talking with another inmate or a family member during a visit or call. Try taking a few deep breaths—fill your stomach with air, hold it for a couple of seconds, and then slowly let it out.
- **Choose the Right Time:**
  - Timing matters. Pick a time when both of you are calm. If you need to, step away to collect your thoughts. Approaching things calmly helps keep the situation from getting worse.
- **Acknowledge Positives:**
  - Start by noticing something positive. Pointing out positives can improve the conversation, whether it's something you see in the other person's behavior or just recognizing their effort.
- **Ask for Their Input:**
  - Even in prison, where choices are limited, asking others for their opinions on decisions that affect them can make them feel respected. It shows you value their input, even if the conversation is difficult.

- **Listen Actively:**
    - You don't have to agree with everything someone says, but it's important to let them know you've listened. Just feeling heard can help calm things down and lead to better understanding.
- **Acknowledge Struggles:**
    - If the person you're talking to seems to be struggling, gently tell them you see that. Show your support without judgment. These small actions can help them feel supported rather than attacked.
- **Express Your Needs Clearly:**
    - Be sure to communicate clearly. Say it directly if you need something from someone, like respect, space, or understanding.
- **Create a Calming Atmosphere:**
    - Keeping things calm in prison can be challenging, but try to create a peaceful atmosphere when possible. This might mean speaking softly, avoiding aggressive body language, or making eye contact to show respect. These small actions can help prevent conflicts from getting worse.

These tips can make talking with others more manageable, even in prison. You can improve your communication by staying calm, picking the right time to talk, and showing respect. Listen carefully, recognize others' feelings, and be clear about what you need. Doing these things can help build better understanding, respect, and support, making your interactions more positive.

Use the following pages to practice and improve how you talk with others. These exercises are designed to help you communicate more effectively, handle tough situations, and build better connections. Take your time with each activity, and try to use the tips we've talked about. This will help you have clearer and more positive conversations.

Use the questions below to help you gather your thoughts.

Who do I want to talk to, and why?

Example: "I want to talk to my cellmate about sharing space more respectfully. I want this talk because I want us both to feel respected in our space."

Am I calm enough to have this conversation right now?

Example: "I feel frustrated but can take a deep breath and approach the conversation calmly." Or "I need more time to think before this conversation."

What positive things have I noticed about this person that I can share in the conversation?

Example: "My cellmate helped me last week when I needed it."

Plan how you will start and handle the conversation.

What time and place will I choose for this conversation?

Example: During recreation time when we're both more relaxed.

How can I involve them in the conversation and ask for their input?

Example: "How do you feel about the way we're sharing our space?"

After you have your conversation, reflect on how it went.

Did I actively listen to their perspective? What did I hear them say?

Example: They said they've been feeling stressed, too, which I didn't realize.

How did I acknowledge their struggles without judgment?

____

____

Example: "I get that you're under a lot of pressure too."

Did I clearly express my needs? What were they?

____

____

Example: I expressed that I need a little more personal space in the mornings.

How can you continue to improve your communication skills?

What went well in this conversation?

____

____

Example: I stayed calm and listened to what they had to say.

What could I do better next time?

____

____

Example: I could give them more space to explain their perspective before jumping in.

Reflect on the Conversation

Take some time to think through the conversation. Write down what went well, something new you learned about the other person and something new you learned about yourself.

Example: I noticed that staying calm helped the conversation go better. I also learned that my cellmate has their own problems, and now I feel more understanding towards them.

Icebreakers

Icebreaker questions are simple, fun questions that help start conversations. You can use them with other inmates or with your loved ones during phone calls or visits.

- What is your favorite color?
- Who is your favorite superhero?
- Do you drink the milk after you eat cereal?
- If your family was a sitcom, which one would they be?
- What was your favorite book as a child?
- If you could pick a superpower what would it be?
- Would you want to find out when you are going to die?
- Cats or Dogs?
- What was your favorite candy as a kid?
- What is your favorite candy now?
- Which holiday is your favorite?
- If you could go to space would you?
- Favorite cartoon? Which character is most like you?
- Favorite cereal?
- Favorite ice cream? Cup or Cone?
- Favorite video game?
- Last time you laughed out loud?
- Favorite Singer? Favorite Song they sing?
- Favorite Actor? Favorite show/movie the were in?
- What is your favorite season and why?
- What is something you are really good at?
- What is something unique about you?

- If you could be friends with anyone famous who would it be?
- Are you a morning person or a night owl?
- Your favorite meal as a kid?
- Cake or cookies?
- Favorite pizza toppings?
- Can you play an instrument?
- What's the funniest joke you've ever heard?
- If you could be any character from a book or movie, who would you be?
- What's the weirdest food you've ever tried?
- If you could be famous for one thing, what would it be?
- What's your favorite sport or outdoor activity?
- If you could have any job when you get out, what would it be?
- If you could have any meal right now, what would it be?
- What's one thing that always makes you feel better, even on tough days?
- Who is someone that inspires you, and why?
- What's something you've done that you're proud of?
- Strangest food you ever ate?
- Would you prefer to be hot or cold?
- What was the name of your stuffed animal as a kid?
- Did you have an imaginary friend?
- Have you broken a bone?
- Best day of your life so far?
- Did you have a favorite teacher? What did she do special?
- If you could take a pill and forget your whole past would you?
- How do you like to celebrate?

Name and Tame: Take Control of Your Emotions

Understanding your emotions can be challenging. The good news is that by naming your emotions, you can better handle them.

Think of your emotions like a messy room. It's hard to know where to start when everything is scattered around. But if you can name what each item is and where it belongs, it becomes easier to clean up.

When you give your emotions a name, it's like putting everything in order. You're not just feeling something—you're understanding what it is. This helps shift your feelings from the part of your brain that reacts automatically to the part that can think things through.

Naming your emotions is like saying, "Yes, I feel this way, and that's okay." It's acknowledging that you have feelings, just like everyone else. What matters is how you choose to handle those feelings. Instead of being overwhelmed by your emotions, you can look at them more clearly and figure out how to deal with them. So, next time you feel an overwhelming emotion, try to name it.

Talking about your feelings can you help you sort them out. Sharing with family members or mental health professionals can bring you support, relief, and understanding.

Writing down your feelings in a journal is a smart move, whether you're happy, excited, sad, or frustrated. When you name your emotions in your own words, it helps you decide how to deal with them in a way that fits what's important to you.

When you say "I feel" followed by your emotions, it helps others understand what you're going through and enables you to respond better.

Take some time to practice using "I feel" statements. Write about times when you feel down or negative and when you feel positive or happy.

I feel

I feel

I feel

I feel

I feel

I feel

I feel

Emotion	Strong	Mild	Come up with your own
Angry	Furious Irate Enraged Infuriated Seething Livid Outraged Fuming Exasperated Boiling	Annoyed Irritated Upset Frustrated Displeased Agitated Cross Bothered Perturbed	
Sad	Devastated Heartbroken Despondent Grief-stricken Sorrowful Distraught Desolate Woeful Inconsolable Mournful Overwhelmed	Blue Down Disappointed Upset Unhappy Glum Gloomy Bummed Sad Flat Low	
Happy	Ecstatic Elated Overjoyed Thrilled Exhilarated Radiant Jubilant Delighted Exuberant Blissful Beaming Enthusiastic Rapturous	Content Cheerful Pleased Joyful Glad Bright Upbeat Sunny Smiling Satisfied Lighthearted Merry Comfortable	

Staying in Control

Planning how to manage your emotions, can help you deal with tough situations in prison. Your plan can help you control your feelings and actions better, making you feel more at peace and improving your relationships with others.

Here are some helpful tips to help you stay in control.

Mindfulness: When I start feeling worked up, I can take a few deep breaths to help me calm down.

- Instead of letting my mind race, I'll focus on my breathing and stay in the moment. This helps me think more clearly and keeps me from reacting without thinking.

Self-Calming: When I'm feeling stressed or upset, I can do something I enjoy to relax.

- I might draw, listen to music, or read a book. These activities help take my mind off what's bothering me and make me feel more at ease.

Opposite Action: If someone disagrees with me or says something I don't like, I'll try to see things from their point of view.

- I don't have to agree with them, but I can choose to stay calm and not let it turn into a big argument. This way, I keep my cool and avoid trouble.

Use the next page to make a plan for how you'll handle your emotions the next time something upsets you.

Describe a time when something or someone really got to you. What happened? What did they say or do?

____

____

____

____

Example: Another inmate made a disrespectful comment about me in front of others.

What were you feeling when this happened? Were you angry, embarrassed, frustrated?

____

____

____

____

Example: I felt angry, disrespected, and embarrassed.

How did you react? Did you yell, fight, or try to talk it out? What happened because of your reaction?

____

____

____

____

Example: I reacted by getting in the inmate's face and threatening them. We ended up in a fight, and I got put in solitary for a week.

Now, on the following page, think about how you can handle a situation like this in the future.

Mindfulness:

Example: When I start feeling worked up, I can take deep breaths to calm down. I'll focus on my breathing to stay in the moment and think clearly.

Your Mindfulness Plan:

____

____

____

____

Self-Calming:

Example: When I'm stressed or upset, I'll do something I enjoy, like drawing, listening to music, or reading, to relax.

Your Self-Calming Plan:

____

____

____

____

Opposite Action:

Example: If someone disagrees with me, I'll try to see things from their point of view. I don't have to agree, but I'll stay calm and avoid turning it into a fight.

Your Opposite Action Plan:

____

____

____

____

Remember:

Having a plan doesn't mean you won't ever feel angry or upset—it just helps you stay in control when you do. Use your plan to keep yourself focused, calm, and out of trouble.

Simple Exercises for Strength and Fitness

Exercise should challenge you and help you get stronger, but it shouldn't hurt. Listen to your body and recognize the difference between feeling tired and actual pain, which could mean you're injured. If you're new to working out or have health issues, talk to a doctor before starting a routine to make sure it's safe and right for you. Here's a workout plan you can try. It's all bodyweight exercises you can do without any equipment, even in a small space. Use the exercise log to track your progress and increase your reps as you get stronger.

Day One: Upper Body Strength

- **Close-Grip Push-Ups**
    - Perform a push-up with your hands closer together, under your chest, to focus more on the triceps.

  Target: Triceps, chest, shoulders

- **Dips**
    - Use a sturdy chair or bed edge.
    - Place your hands on the edge, facing forward, and lower your body by bending your elbows.
    - Push back up.

  Target: Triceps, shoulders, chest

- **Pike Push-Ups**
    - Start in a downward dog position.
    - Lower your head toward the ground by bending your elbows.
    - Push back up.

  Target: Shoulders, upper chest

- **Bicep Hold:**
    - Clench both hands into fists.
    - Push your fists together in front of your chest.
    - Push your fists against each other as hard as you can.
    - Keep this tension for 10-20 seconds, then release.

  Target: Biceps

- **Diamond Push-Ups**
    - Do a push-up with your hands in a diamond shape under your chest to target your triceps.

  Target: Triceps, chest

Day Two: Full Body Strength

- **Push-Ups**
  - Start in a plank position.
  - Position your hands shoulder-width apart.
  - Lower your body to the floor until your chest almost touches the floor.
  - Push back up to the starting position.

  Target: Chest, shoulders, triceps, and core

  Modifications: Use your knees or do push-ups against a wall.

- **Squats**
  - Stand with feet shoulder-width apart.
  - Place your hands behind your head.
  - Bend your knees to lower yourself until your thighs are parallel to the ground.
  - Push back up to the starting position.

  Target: Legs, glutes, core

- **Plank**
  - Lay on the ground on your stomach.
  - Put your forearms on the ground and push up using your arms and toes so the only thing touching the floor are your forearms and toes.
  - Keep your body in a straight line from head to heels.
  - Hold this position, engaging your core.

  Target: Core, shoulders, back

  Modifications: Hold the plank from your knees.

- **Superman Hold**
  - Lie face down on the floor with your arms stretched out in front of you.
  - Lift your arms, chest, and legs off the floor at the same time.
  - Hold the position for a few seconds, keeping your body straight and your head in a neutral position.
  - Slowly lower your arms, chest, and legs back down to the floor.

  Target: Lower back, glutes

Day Three: Cardio & Core

- **<u>High Knees</u>**
  - Jog in place while driving your knees as high as possible, lifting them towards your chest.

  Target: Cardio, legs, core

- **<u>Mountain Climbers</u>**
  - Start in a plank position.
  - Bring one knee toward your chest, then switch legs in a running motion while keeping your hands on the floor.

  Target: Core, shoulders, cardio

- **<u>Bicycle Crunches</u>**
  - Lie on your back.
  - Lift your legs, and alternate bringing your elbow toward the opposite knee in a twisting motion.

  Target: Core, obliques

- **<u>Leg Raises</u>**
  - Lie on your back with your legs straight.
  - Lift your legs toward the ceiling, keeping them as straight as possible.
  - Lower them back down without letting them touch the floor.

  Target: Lower abs

- **<u>Russian Twists</u>**
  - Sit on the floor with your knees bent and feet off the ground.
  - Twist your torso from side to side, tapping the floor on each side.

  Target: Core, obliques

- **<u>Jumping Jacks</u>**
  - Start standing with your feet together and arms by your side.
  - Jump your feet out while raising your arms overhead, then jump back to the starting position.

  Target: Full-body cardio

Day Four: Mobility & Flexibility

- **Cat-Cow Stretch**
    - Start on your hands and knees.
    - Arch your back upward (cat pose).
    - Drop your belly down while lifting your head and tailbone (cow pose).

  Target: Spine, back, core flexibility

- **Hip Flexor Stretch**
    - Step one leg forward into a lunge position.
    - Keep your back leg straight and front knee bent at 90 degrees.
    - Hold the stretch.

  Target: Hip flexors, thighs

- **Shoulder Stretch**
    - Bring one arm across your chest.
    - Use your opposite arm to gently press it towards your body.

  Target: Shoulders

- **Hamstring Stretch**
    - Sit on the floor with one leg extended straight.
    - Bend your other leg, resting your foot against your inner thigh.
    - Reach for your toes on the extended leg.

  Target: Hamstrings, lower back

- **Downward Dog**
    - Start on all fours.
    - Lift your hips toward the ceiling.
    - Straighten your legs and arms to form an inverted V-shape with your body.

  Target: Hamstrings, calves, shoulders

- **Child's Pose**
    - Get down on the floor with your hands and knees on the mat.
    - Move your knees apart, keeping your big toes touching.
    - Gently sit your hips back towards your heels.
    - Stretch your arms out in front of you, letting your forehead rest on the mat.
    - Breathe deeply and let your body relax in this position.

  Target: Lower back, shoulders, hips

Day Five: Lower Body Strength

- **Squat Jumps**
  - Do a squat.
  - Jump upward, landing softly.
  - Go back into a squat.

  Target: Legs, glutes, cardio

- **Glute Bridges**
  - Lie on your back with your knees bent.
  - Lift your hips off the floor by squeezing your glutes.
  - Lower back down.

  Target: Glutes, hamstrings

- **Step-Ups**
  - Use a bench or a sturdy platform to step up with one foot, driving through your heel to lift your body.
  - Step back down.

  Target: Legs, glutes

- **Wall Sit**
  - Stand against a wall.
  - Slide down into a squat position with your back against the wall.
  - Hold the position.

  Target: Legs, glutes

- **Calf Raises**
  - Stand on your toes, lifting your heels off the ground.
  - Lower back down.

  Target: Calves

- **Side Lunges**
  - Step to the side and lower your body into a lunge position, keeping the opposite leg straight.

  Target: Legs, glutes, inner thighs

Day Six: Cardio & Core

- **High Knees**
    - Same as day three

  Target: Full body, cardio

- **Jumping Jacks**
    - Same as day three

  Target: Full-body cardio

- **Flutter Kicks**
    - Lie on your back with your legs straight out.
    - Lift your legs slightly off the ground and alternate kicking them up and down.

  Target: Core, lower abs

- **Plank with Leg Raises**
    - Get in a plank position.
    - Raise one leg a few inches off the ground, keeping the rest of your body still.
    - Lower that leg and lift the other one, keeping your body steady.

  Target: Core, glutes

- **Reverse Crunches**
    - Lie on your back with your legs bent.
    - Lift your hips off the ground as you bring your knees toward your chest.

  Target: Lower abs

- **Skaters**
    - Start by standing with your feet shoulder-width apart.
    - Push off with your right foot and jump to your left, landing on your left foot. As you jump, swing your arms to help with balance—your right arm swings forward when you jump to the left.
    - Now, push off with your left foot and jump to your right, landing on your right foot.
    - Keep jumping side to side, staying low and balanced like a speed skater.

  Target: Cardio, legs, balance

Day Seven: Rest / Active Recovery

Take a few minutes to stretch on your rest day.

WORKOUT LOG

Goals: ____________________

Date: ________ ________ ________ ________

Weight: ________ ________ ________ ________

Stats: ________ ________ ________ ________

Exercise:	*Sets*	*Reps*	*Wt*	*Sets*	*Reps*	*Wt*	*Sets*	*Reps*	*Wt*	*Sets*	*Reps*	*Wt*

Cardio Exercise:	*Time*	*Dist.*	*Int.*	*Time*	*Dist.*	*Int.*	*Time*	*Dist.*	*Int.*	*Time*	*Dist.*	*Int.*

Notes:

WORKOUT LOG

Goals: ____________________

Date: ________ ________ ________ ________

Weight: ________ ________ ________ ________

Stats: ________ ________ ________ ________

Exercise:	*Sets*	*Reps*	*Wt*	*Sets*	*Reps*	*Wt*	*Sets*	*Reps*	*Wt*	*Sets*	*Reps*	*Wt*

Cardio Exercise:	*Time*	*Dist.*	*Int.*	*Time*	*Dist.*	*Int.*	*Time*	*Dist.*	*Int.*	*Time*	*Dist.*	*Int.*

Notes:

Unlock New Worlds Through Reading

Reading is a simple way to give your mind a break and step away from your current situation. It lets you visit new places, discover new ideas, and see things in a new light.

- Challenge yourself to read different kinds of books—if you usually read non-fiction, why not try fiction?
- You could start a book club with someone on the outside or in your unit. Talking about stories, characters, and ideas can be a nice break from your surroundings.
- If you like visuals with your reading, try graphic novels.

Browse through the books available to you in the prison. Here are some ideas to help you begin your reading journey.

Fiction Books:

- **"Long Way Down"** by Jason Reynolds (also available as a graphic novel)
- **"The Fault in Our Stars"** by John Green
- **"The Catcher in the Rye"** by J.D. Salinger
- **"The Kite Runner"** by Khaled Hosseini
- **"The Outsiders"** by S.E. Hinton
- **"Lord of the Flys"** by William Golding
- **"Altered Childhood"** or **"Donuts and Deceit,"** by P.B Alden (AKA Patricia & Beth!)
- Any book by Stephen King, John Grisham, or Frederick Backman.

Non-Fiction Books:

- **"Born a Crime"** by Trevor Noah
- **"Atomic Habits"** by James Clear
- **"Unfu*k Yourself"** by Gary John Bishop
- **"Daring Greatly"** by Brené Brown (or any of her other books)
- **"The Power of Now"** by Eckhart Tolle
- **"Man's Search for Meaning"** by Viktor E. Frankl
- **"You Are a Badass"** by Jen Sincero
- **"The Subtle Art of Not Giving a F*ck"** by Mark Manson
- **"Grit"** by Angela Duckworth

Use the following page to chart your reading and watch your world open up.

My Reading List

My Favorites

Creative Doodling
Fun Ways to Draw For Any Skill Level

You don't need to be an artist to enjoy doodling or drawing—just grab a pencil and some paper, and you're ready to go. In this section, we'll go over five easy pencil techniques. One of the best things about using pencils is that you can create different shades by pressing harder or softer. Unlike markers, where it's tough to change how light or dark your lines are, pencils make it easy to smoothly go from light to dark with just a bit of pressure. These tips and techniques are about having fun and seeing what you can create, no matter your skill level. So jump in and start drawing!

Blended Fade

- Press the pencil on the paper to create a light, soft line.
- Gradually press a little harder to make the line darker.
- Practice going from light to dark in one stroke by slowly increasing the pressure as you draw.
- You can use the tip of your finger to smudge the pencil marks and create smooth shading.
- Try shading a simple shape like a circle by starting light on one side and gradually pressing harder as you move to the other.

Scumbling

- Hold your pencil and use small, circular motions to make marks on the paper.
- Try pressing lightly for lighter shades and harder for darker shades as you draw.
- Draw lots of small circles close together. The more you overlap them, the darker the shading will become.
- Experiment with different patterns of circles or scribbles to make your own unique design.

Crosshatching, Hatching, or Stippling

- Use your pencil to make small, short lines or dashes on your paper.
- Create patterns by adding crossed lines or dots in the areas you want to shade.
- Keep adding these marks to fill in sections of your drawing with varying shades.
- Try using these marks to form shapes, letters, or unique designs for a creative touch.

Burnishing

- Use your pencil to make small, solid patches or areas on your paper by moving your pencil back and forth.
- Press down as hard as you can without breaking your pencil tip.
- Keep going until those patches look shiny and smooth.
- This technique works great for drawing shiny things like ceramics or glass.

Directional Lines

- Look at an object you've drawn and pay attention to how it moves or flows.
- Use smooth, swooping lines that follow this movement to highlight certain parts of your artwork. This helps make your drawing feel like it's moving and shows people where to look.
- To make it more interesting, gently change how hard you press the pencil as you draw these lines. This adds depth and makes your drawing look more detailed and exciting.

Eraser Drawing

- Shade the whole paper with a medium pencil color.
- Use the eraser to remove some of the pencil shading, revealing the white paper underneath.
- Press harder with your pencil to draw dark outlines around the white areas, making parts of your drawing stand out.

Transferred Symmetry

- Fold a piece of paper in half.
- Starting at the folded line, use your pencil to press down hard and draw one-half of a shape that is the same on both sides, like a butterfly or a face.
- Next, fold the paper back over.
- Rub the paper's outside with the pencil body's hard side to transfer your drawing to the other side.
- Open the paper and retrace the transferred image. Now, you can design your symmetrical drawing!

Pencil Texture Rubbings

- Put a textured object under your paper—like a rough concrete surface or woven fabric.
- Use the side of your pencil and rub it over the paper where the textured object is underneath.
- Experiment with different textures to create a complete picture.

Torn Paper Smearing

- Tear a piece of paper to create an interesting edge or shape.
- Place the torn edge on your drawing paper.
- Use your pencil to draw dark lines around the edge of the torn shape.
- Then, use your finger to smudge the pencil marks, spreading the graphite outward from the edge to create a soft, smeared halo effect.

Single Line Drawing

- Start drawing on the surface of your paper without lifting your pencil.
- Create a scene or interesting shapes using one continuous line.
- Keep your pencil on the paper until your drawing is complete.
- Enjoy your unique creation!

You can use the examples provided or come up with your own drawings.
Have fun trying out these techniques to create artwork
that shows your unique style!

1
2
3
4
5
6

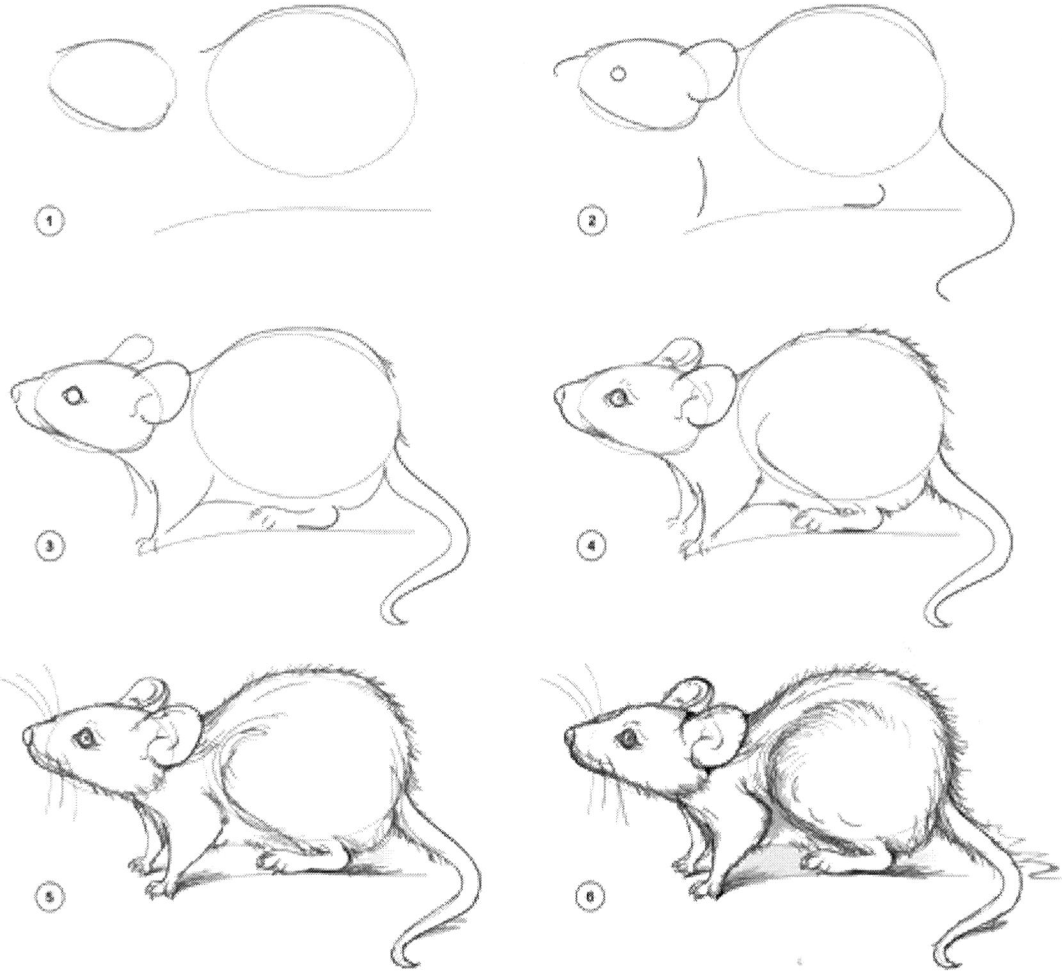
1
2
3
4
5
6

1
2
3
4
5
6
7
8
9

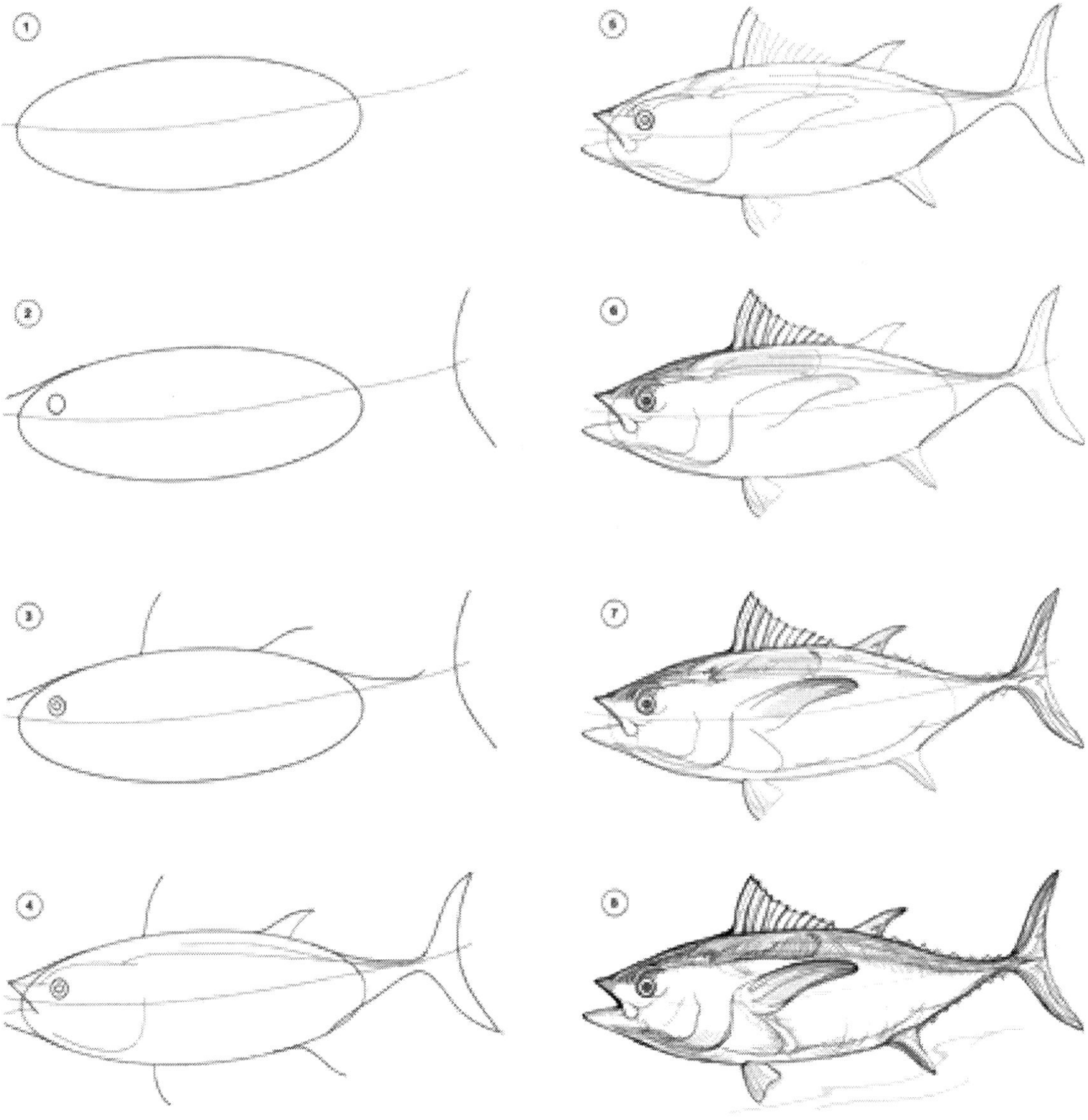
1
2
3
4
5
6
7
8

1
2
3
4
5
6
7
8

1

2

3

4

5

6

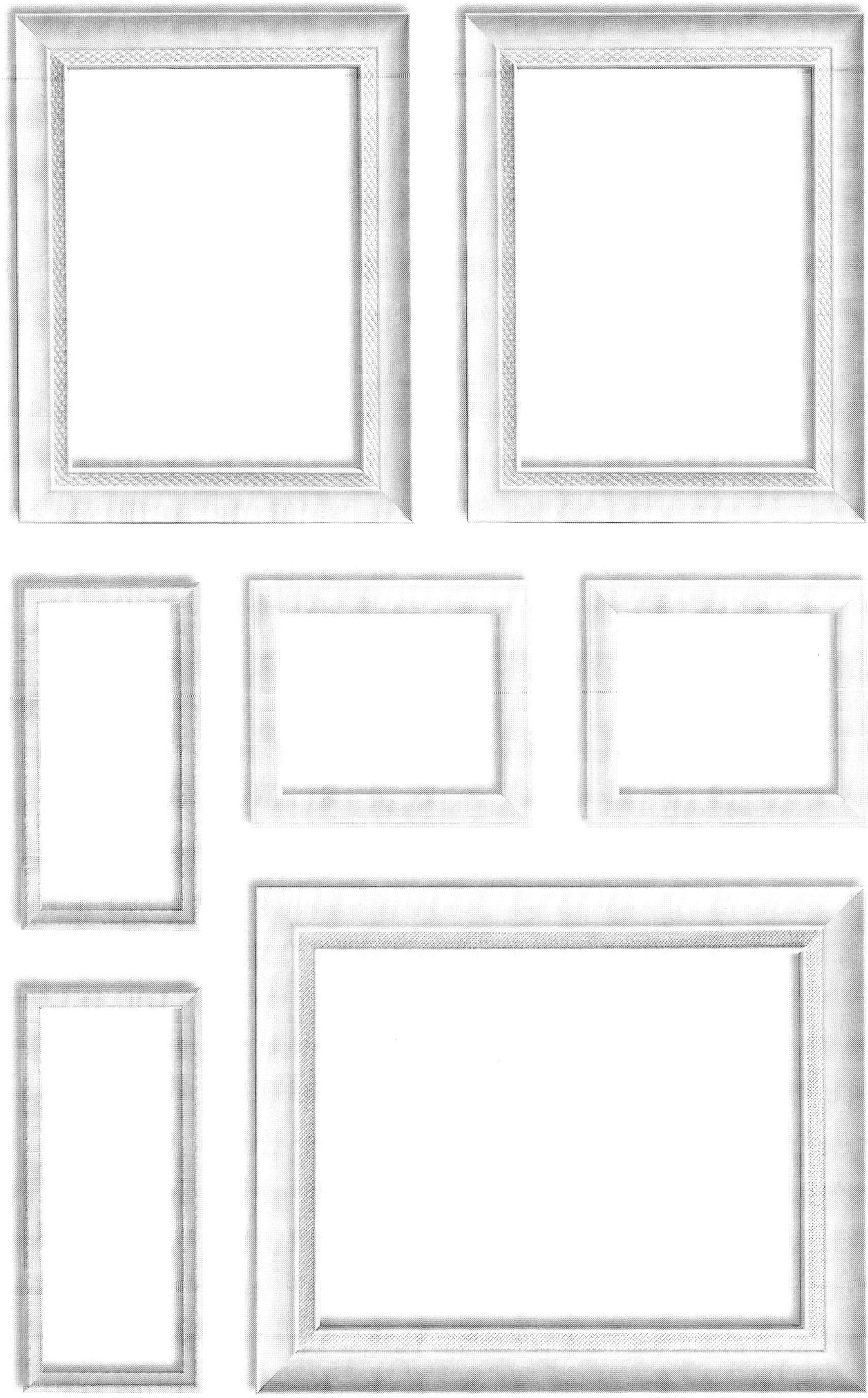

Puzzles

Find Two Identical Pictures

Puzzle 1

Find Two Identical Pictures

Puzzle 2

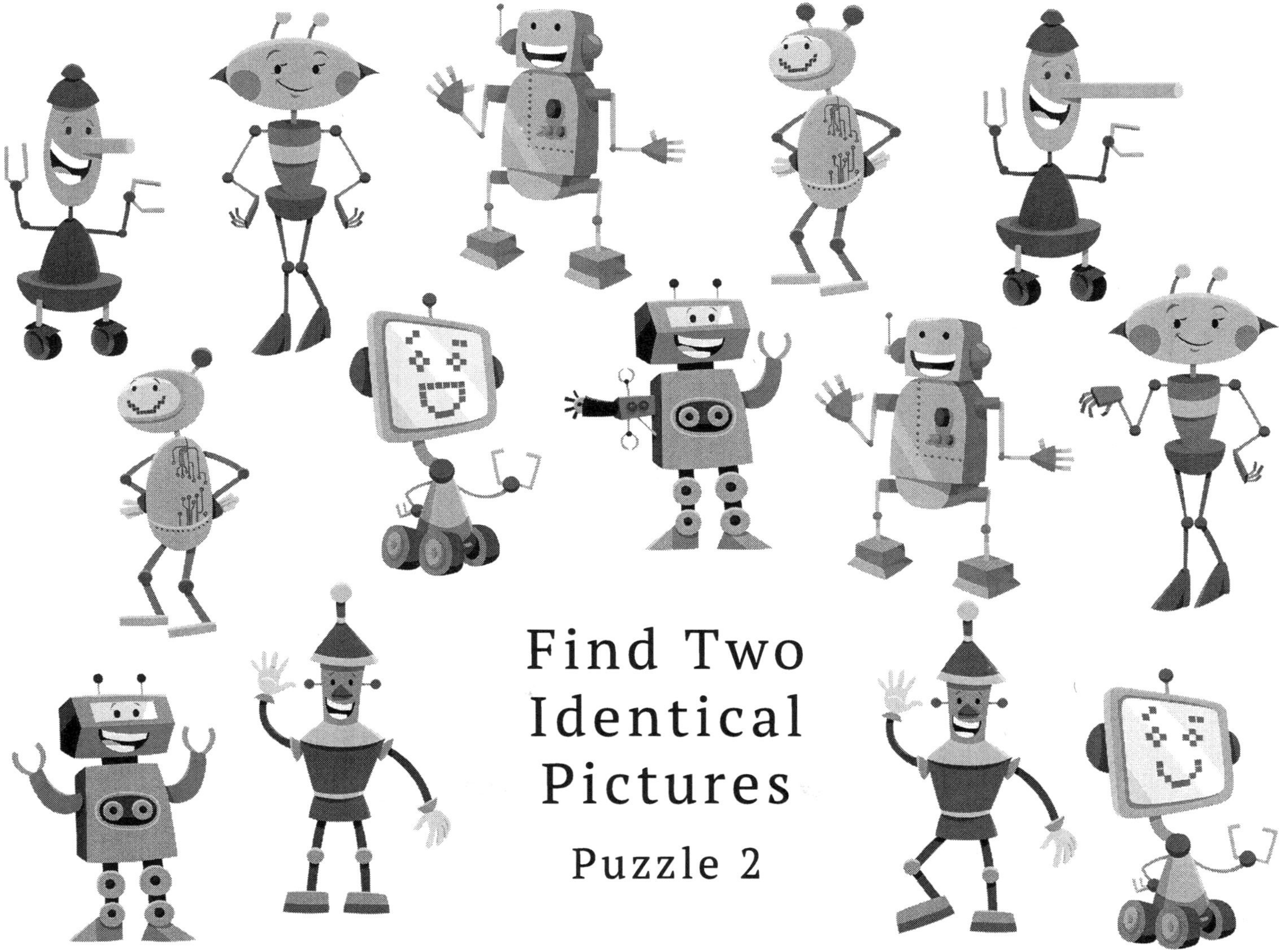

Find Two Identical Pictures

Puzzle 3

Find Two Identical Pictures

Puzzle 4

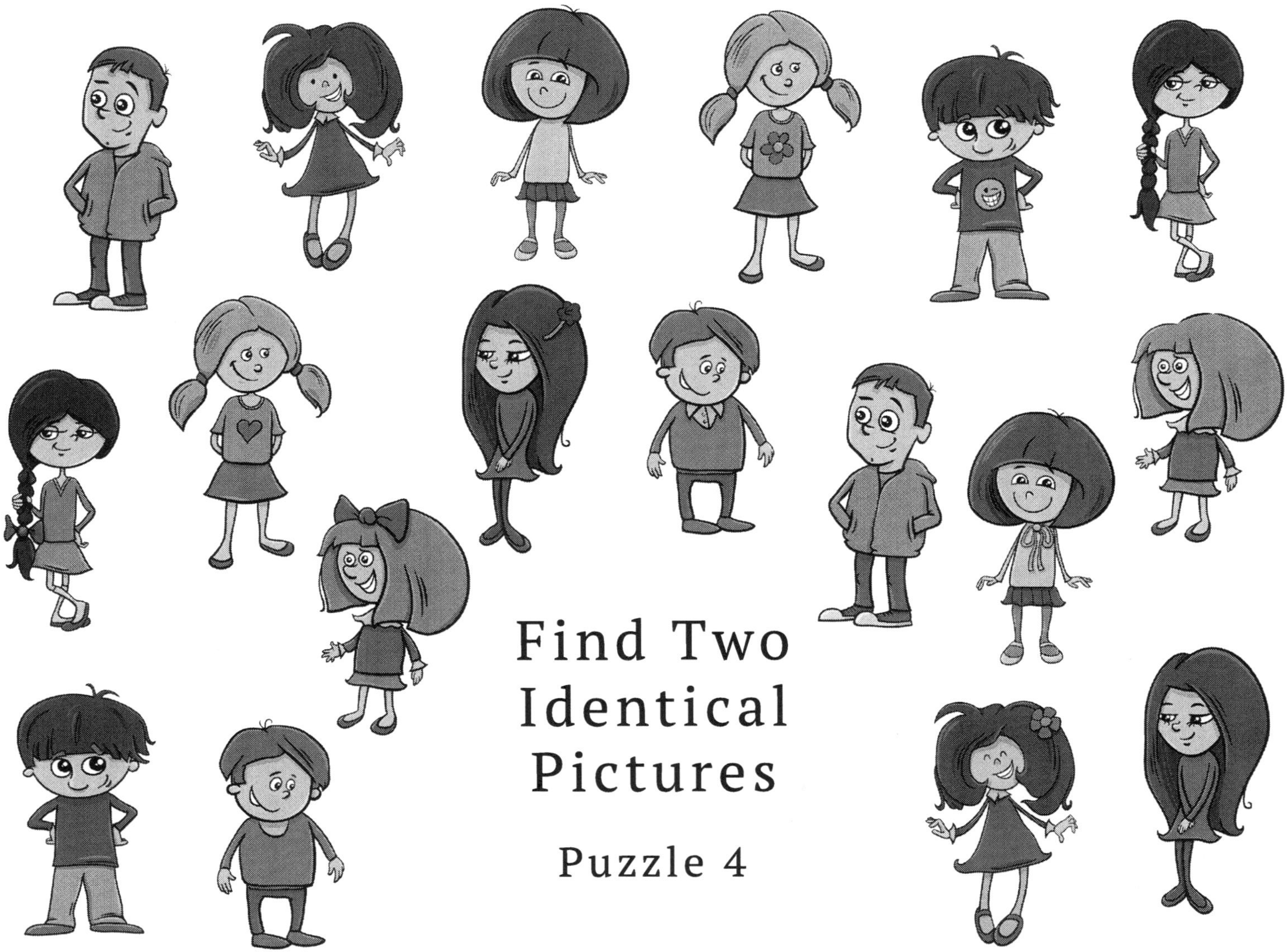

Find 10 Differences
Puzzle 5

Find 8 Differences
Puzzle 6

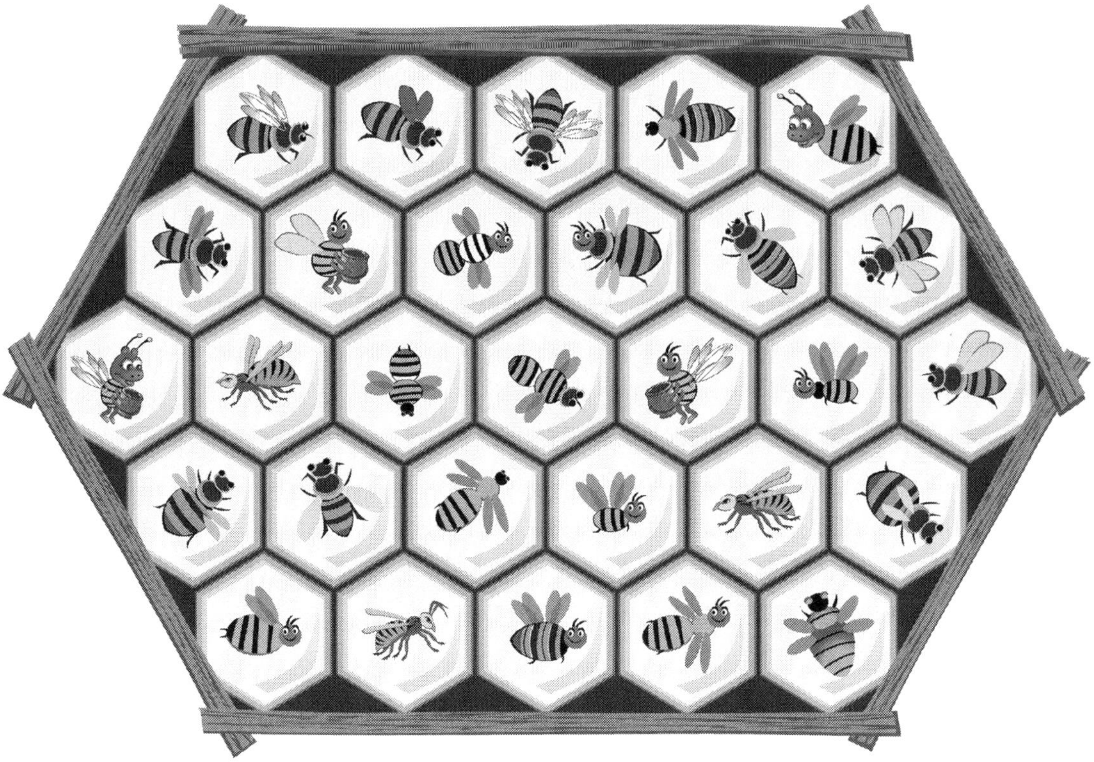

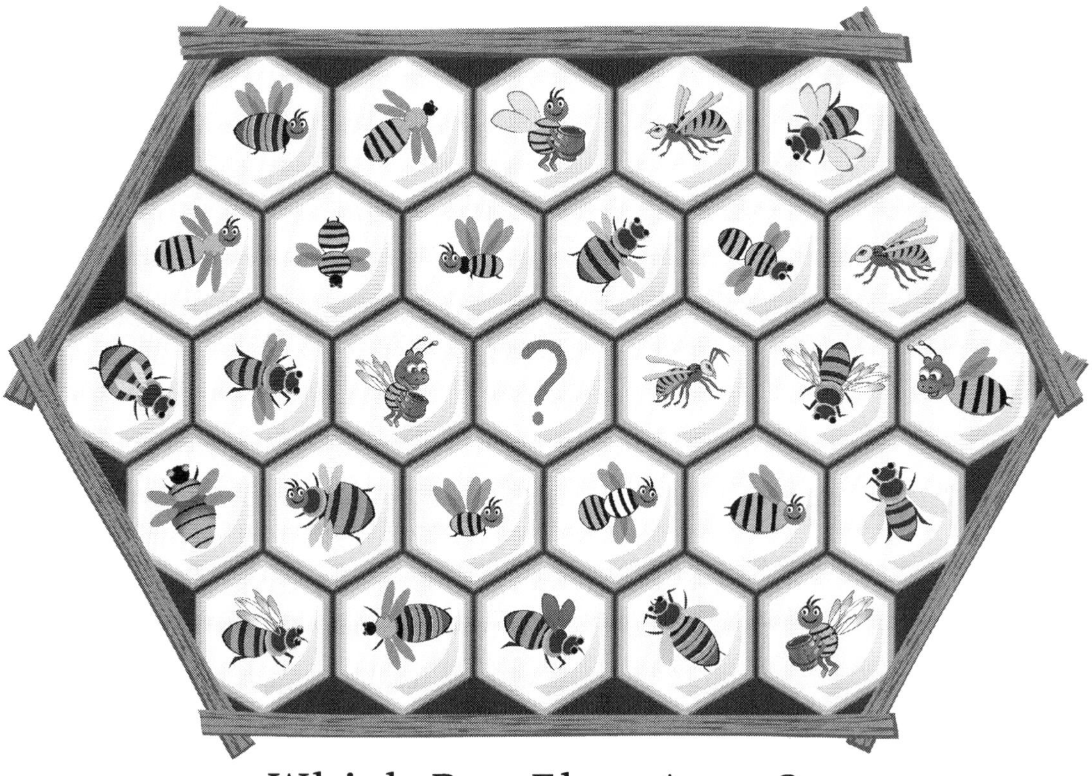

Which Bee Flew Away?
Puzzle 7

Find Identical
Puzzle 8

Image Puzzle Answers

Puzzle1

Puzzle 2

Puzzle 3

Puzzle 4

Puzzle 5

Puzzle 6

Puzzle 7

Puzzle 8

Candy Bars

Y C M R G O O D B A R S F R R
R A A
N K K I N D E R B U E N O B B
E O B A S
H M Y A W Y K L I M V P H K R
H B K V W N A
O Q A M P G A L A X Y W O O M
O Y E Z K P E W B
N Z R G Y S J H B N C K N S M
E T O N T F Q D U L U
S O D U Y F U O B H X O T N S
T B A C I F O P Q V R O K
L L L Y R Z B I S O U E A H E
E E M H L P S W G X V B G T T
C R O E I L G L V I H A E A E
R O N L N D E N P A R O R E
U N D N D A V R R L R G U A R
N E J U T V A O L S M S
C U O N I G P I Z C K E S O Z
H Q Y W Y S R Y O G
A Y M J F M Z E K O S K A N T
S T T L O D U A
R N Y G R A B H T A E H Y I K
E U N A Q T
K O O H T U R Y B A B N P F I
C B B K
I D D U P S O H A D I E N S O
N R
S D D E K A H S K L I M H X C

WORD LIST:

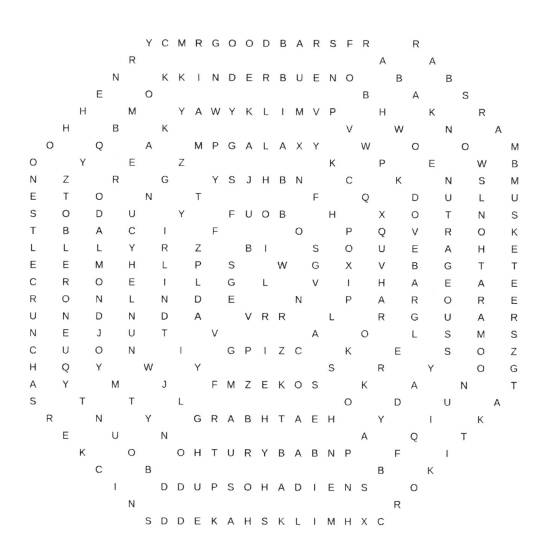

AERO
ALMOND JOY
BABY RUTH
BOUNTY
DOVE BAR
GALAXY
HEATH BAR
IDAHO SPUD
KINDER BUENO
KIT KAT
LINDT
MARATHON
MARS BAR
MILK SHAKE
MILKY WAY
MR GOODBAR
MUSKETEERS
NESTLE CRUNCH
NUTRAGEOUS
OH HENRY
PAYDAY
SKOR
SNICKERS
TOBLERONE
WONKA BAR

I am calm

l	i	m	p	i	d	b	r	t	c	k	b	u	q	e	o	d	t	r	h
t	r	a	n	q	u	i	l	a	g	v	e	h	v	v	g	t	z	v	f
c	o	o	l	h	e	a	d	e	d	d	j	z	u	m	l	b	t	t	w
y	r	d	u	i	e	m	s	e	r	e	n	e	e	o	u	e	p	o	s
c	s	t	i	l	l	e	r	x	i	l	q	q	k	l	u	d	v	n	i
o	h	a	u	b	w	e	n	o	q	u	n	t	r	o	u	b	l	e	d
o	g	z	c	o	m	p	o	s	e	d	a	w	y	f	g	e	q	l	l
l	k	r	w	r	w	j	x	n	z	k	i	h	p	c	d	s	x	g	o
q	s	y	w	b	x	w	y	x	q	d	t	r	a	n	q	u	i	l	h
u	p	e	a	c	e	f	u	l	s	e	r	e	n	e	i	t	r	a	o
i	v	b	j	m	c	a	z	x	x	o	m	s	x	z	q	c	e	e	i
e	m	a	z	u	d	u	n	d	i	s	t	u	r	b	e	d	n	p	u
t	f	u	c	f	c	t	n	t	j	w	f	r	e	l	a	x	e	d	e
n	t	n	a	n	q	o	i	u	j	z	d	h	s	a	d	h	h	h	o
i	g	h	l	z	g	g	d	c	o	l	l	e	c	t	e	d	p	p	i
z	n	j	m	b	s	e	e	o	r	f	t	h	t	d	g	l	v	x	r
h	f	x	s	e	l	t	q	s	c	e	h	r	k	f	q	x	t	h	c
q	a	f	p	o	r	h	d	u	n	r	u	f	f	l	e	d	w	o	d
e	y	o	m	w	m	e	a	j	v	z	h	e	j	f	a	y	f	g	y
x	e	y	n	i	v	r	p	y	o	u	v	h	a	r	m	o	n	y	u

undisturbed	untroubled	coolheaded	unruffled
collected	tranquil	together	peaceful
tranquil	relaxed	serene	harmony
limpid	serene	still	level
composed	quiet	calm	cool

Dogs are number 1

C

K H

D P O

A E O W

L S S M C

M H P E E H

A A O Q N R O

T R O C B A A W

I P D G H U V N B

A E L U N I L A I N

N I E P Y H L H A N

U T S N A

A E T O M

H R B O R

U R E P E

A I R I B

E E N T O

G R A L D

S B R A U

H U D M B

I L D R D

B L N O R

A D U T E

I O O T H

N G H W P

U R Y E E

U E E I H

Z V R L S

T E G E N

H I O R A

I R V D M

G T X T Y H T N N R D X I X V

R E X O B S E E X E Y K S U H

I C C M L Q R M V G T Q M E R

WORD LIST:

BOXER
BULLDOG
BULL TERRIER
CHIHUAHUA
CHOW CHOW
DALMATIAN
DOBERMANN
GERMAN SHEPHERD
GREYHOUND
HAVANESE
HUSKY
MALTIPOO
POMERANIAN
POODLE
PUG
RETRIEVER
ROTTWEILER
SHAR PEI
SHIBA INU
SHIH TZU
ST BERNARD

I'm happy

J J D O G Y D A T K
S B Q E G D E X A L E R Q R
H O J G L Y A W K C H I A S H E C J
C Q K P L U F L Z U Y G O A N L P B O I
D P B W I E F P Z E S H P U S U F P F L V P
A L A X R N X E V V O X I U L C K H
F G Y L H T U V W P I X I H D Y K P H
D G H T G M P T H L A L B C U A J B R I
F N P D P F I B K R E E T N P H Y L B V Z U
S C L N X F P E G Y A G U D T F V O G Q W I
H D J D J W V D A E Q S D N M L Z F H P G A Z I
H V R Y V P B Y T I S A W A C C S U M K X F B W
U F C P O U W Q H X F N C L N A L M V R L I H C
D Z Y P Z Z S A M W C D I T T Q W K J W T A M L X V C R O H
C N N A A Z W M I C F D D D R B J I M I Y B P A C M L N M G
I D B H G C M H C R W Q W Y Q Z T J S K V M Y C L D T A N S
C B I L Z Q N W U X F S U Q B R X F C Q X N T E E E N W R D
Z V P E G L E E F U L U M V X L I U I N Z G G B N U F R W C
V A E V O J W M X T G W A M E L A Z Z O O F T K J G O S
P W A Z M X Y K K Y W U D N D R N Q P F T C J E W K
Y C O H X P F U R A Y O J B Y P Q A Q M Y E Q
N E W N A K D Q O P
J B B A V K E W D N
M Q J V P W Q T Y L W X
A U E W C D E S S E L B R B W P N M G H E D Q D
R W Y U K P N X Q O J T D Z M A F G F C N C
N A C A U E W X F Z Y G P Y I I P D N D
T A A Y K D R A A B T N A L I B U J
D E T A L E Y E H P E K M C
K U H K I O Q D U F

WORD LIST:

BLESSED	ELATED	JOY	PLEASANT
CALM	GLAD	JUBILANT	RELAXED
CHIPPER	GLEEFUL	LIVELY	SATISFIED
CONTENT	HAPPY	LUCKY	THRILLED
DELIGHTED	JOLLY	PEACE	UPBEAT

Birds

H C T G K R A F B G
N V N G Z X E K U N Y K W A
O O V A K O Y Z S B V M T A Y Q Q W
H I F G K M O Y L T I O H P W E C E J T
O J U V M V K S P O R C S B D D D C G R D Y
W Y E R K P Y F E T B E F U L W I J O R A V X S
E N F Y W S X O H Z L Y L Z F Q C H R Z O T F L F
C M W W S P A R R O W A R F R N L A I K U V M M L F
V S J X K W O O D C O C K A K H E C Q R T S Z G A Y I A
U W X G J T C C D B S M Q W X Q L Z D R D E K S S C H M
T L A S O W L O O V K K B W D T E R N B S P I C W L A P H T
R T N E L A H O N F H E R O N B I T T E R N B N K P T R H K
M U G I D J H T U P O G Y J O D V P N Z W T R W A B C D S Z
B R B D F B L Z N I P Q D O V E B A Y W C Y N H R L H H P T
E E D J I A D H I G Q A U P F F I T Z G J J C U A A E T O E
A E O J N R S Z V E P N V C A C A P W T U R P M V K R N O A
T J U K C B Z D L O Y A Z T L Y J X R V P D H M E H L B N L
Y U V L H Q C R G N X S E W C E B A X J C H E I N U X Q B U
V O N D V P K Z T H S P H T O T B A G G H I A N Q W T P I K
O Z Y V G R T U E X A S R K N R X L L S Y W S G O Z U Z L X
B G C L N N B G V N U Y L B K O A J D K L A B F F G B L
L D R A C U A R D D A V B M R J B W L E P N I M A I B F
Q B U R T T E K P E Q S N I P E I I N A T R I N G T
O Y B O Y P T O I C R T U R K E Y N X R G D Q J A R
W U W T V N D P F Z M E R G A N S E R D L M J N
L N M V I J E C B L U E B I R D Q I O L E K
V K A Q U R K K W L Q S A D J Z C V H J
Y G U H A W K F L A M I N G O C L K
F L X C H I C K A D E E W W
V O U R Z D S T Q I

BALDEAGLE	EGRET	HUMMINGBIRD	SNIPE
BITTERN	FALCON	KESTREL	SPARROW
BLUEBIRD	FLAMINGO	MERGANSER	SPOONBILL
BOBWHITE	FLYCATCHER	OWL	SWAN
CARDINAL	GOLDFINCH	PHEASANT	TEAL
CHICKADEE	GOOSE	PIGEON	TERN
COOT	GROUSE	RAVEN	TURKEY
CROW	HAWK	ROBIN	VULTURE
DOVE	HERON	SANDPIPER	WOODCOCK

Chips

```
                    F P K P W A V C V I
                L V C X O C Q S L Y I Y W Z
            K I N C A P O M H A J F L B D G I C
          Q N T V L C L R V W P M C W K Z M V W E
        U Q N G Y H G W C Z O T A T O P T E E W S V
      C A V D V I         H K Q G G G       W V L E I Q
    A V W P B P R         E L Q A J G       M R L Z T Q
    U A Z Z S K N         X T W R T J       W S S P T C Q
  C U S M S U S W         M Y X D X M       V O A R A N F W
  P D R L N N F A         I M E E I B       N T N I K Z Q H
M T P Q P U C J R         X W I N D U       I I A N I O J T O
D F K G C Y H S P         U S D O F G       G R N G S R V N B
G D E P Y N I X O         O T O F P L       H F A L V P W A D
L J P A B U P G I T S V W F J E E E Z M V H G B E S C R J T
W E S R I F S Q O G I M O J D A I S N M G I E Q S H B A B Y
K Y B R I K R Z Z H Q T R B V T Z U B V X K H X E E Q Z R T
Z Q E E R U F F L E S W S X W I E E O W V H I E C H O R R P
I K E T T L E S R N V S N O G N S K I A W K T U F S U P O Z
I C I V I   C S K Z J T O J T U R Y R N P O E C   A T F Q X
G J H A P     M C G H J V W M U C Q A P S K C     A H W N H
  J E E N       C X G F W T M R K H A L S D O     N D E M
  E R S D E                                     B O H R W
    R I Q D C                                 Z R O R I
    S W P B A F                             E I M I T S
      G S O U R C R E A M A N D O N I O N A T P N R I
        S A R W A D E I Z P O K E R Q Z T O H Z Q H
          W I C C L E P P N Y Y J V J G S D Z G E
            C F S S J H W T L P R W X X L D K V
                S E H E J C G M B O Q W B S
                    Y J A V X J O V J S
```

BANANA
BARBECUE
BUGLES
CHEDDAR
CHEETOS
CHEX MIX
DORITOS
FRITOS
FUNYUNS
GARDEN OF EATIN
HERR'S
KETTLE
LAY'S
POKER
POPCHIPS
PRAWN
PRINGLES
RUFFLES
SOUR CREAM AND ONION
SUNCHIPS
SWEET POTATO
TAKIS
TERRA
TOSTITOS
WISE

Inspiration

E D P E R S E V E R A N C E I

V G E

I F R D R E T C A R A H C W N

G E R C E

R R C O M P A S S I O N G Q R

O U T G R A G

F D W Y N M A E R D Y H V R Y

D N B N F Q J N I

H E C P L K C G Y I C K E O F

S S A N S Q W E G I I

I X D J V J X E M K V N N T X

L L M W T F U V S C E A G

P A I R N I K I U Q U O L N O

M U R B E J Z Y J F C U L I A

O G A Q T U R Y Z H O R A M L

C H T P N W E N I F A H R S

C T I T O V K A Q A D G C E I

A E O E C F E W E N T U

V R N A M M Y O B D U S Z E L

Z J H E T I C D D O

G K Y H J K I Q U F S Y V T Y

F M P B Q U R R

B K G N O I T I B M A D D U K

E K O W T S

L I N E C N E D I F N O C H M

I L G M

E A T T I T U D E P L A R Q S

V Y

E I G G N I K A T H T A E R B

ACCOMPLISH
ADMIRATION
AMBITION
ATTITUDE
BELIEVE
BREATHTAKING
CHALLENGE
CHARACTER
COMPASSION
CONFIDENCE
CONTENT
DETERMINATION
DREAM
ENCOURAGE
ENDURE
ENERGY
FIX
FOCUS
FORGIVE
GOALS
LAUGHTER
PERSEVERANCE
TRUTH

Islands

W

P T

B A G

X A T E F

I H S P D I

I B A L I X B J

T S F M D V C L J W

D O O A M C G F H M P

G M T H S R N F C C H Q O

T T O S I G S V M K C M Z P

X J G B Y B O U H H M X H A X T

C S C A E A J Q C R Q T F R L Y F

W S T T G O N T L A N F R G I R D E F

W A U M O J Q M R V H A G V S J Q I C V

B W Z T F Q B O N A J H O A W U B I L V R F

G T M V U I N X K O X Y A W S M R N Z N E C O

M R F A A H D N K M A P A P S Z M Z S F Y U S S B

Y E W I M R H U M I Q Y K I E O L S Q I V Y U Q O T

V R N I Y J X T T L W P I Q W L Q H M D B G W C H W D J

A X A R Y G V L I P X T L M I L D Q S W H R K P B M G A U

F K Z D K C L V J U N O M Z G Q E A H K R L B V C S W T Y B L

P B E A H F E H E D O I K A D G H D Y D U R O K A T B K S Q R U

S H M D M E O K L V I T I Q G W L C I X F I J A I B C P T Y J E A Q

P U F N L B U H Z A L H E T U J B Y N Q X S Z X P U K C E Z A T K B A

T B K J E A S T E R R U Z D N A E Z E I U W J K B S O E Z M Z X Y Y Z K X

G T E R R V Y M N Y Q O B H U F K L S R Z S O Q U N B N V E C H X L H J D S

V O R T O U L U U V Q T A K X Z N B Z V T T D Q H K U X E C S S V J Y Z E J X Y

T

F

V

R B I B S H J O K K A O I X P S W M C U R A C A O C Y J A W I Z H X R A W T J U

Y O K K G R K F J D S L E G H S E O M J Z K G K Y B R U P L C O Z Z F N R Z

S H R I E U D I N Y A K L A K X F G W M W X U Y B A R O A L H D X B K N L S

R U A K O U E F E P B W I V A G G J X Z P Y H W Z S A R I Y Q H B S K W

N Z X C T L G G K H A G J Q G F T E F T A R U B A E N V C K I B V B N D

S V R A K V U C I I B O R A B O R A F U E M W O H B K V G J E R Q R

N A S A Y J R I Q U D G C A I C O S B V K H U K A N G U I L L A I S

C I Y K P C Z J N I D O I K G M Y G U O V R H F E C U J F H E A

U H U S O G D E U C A R R B Y G I O P X R T D N O X D Z L L R R

WORD LIST:

ANGUILLA	BORABORA	EASTER	MARTINIQUE
ARUBA	BORACAY	FIJI	PHUKET
BAHAMAS	CAICOS	GRENADA	SEYCHELLES
BALI	CEBU	HAWAII	TOBAGO
BARBADOS	CURACAO	MALDIVES	TRINIDAD

Candy Bar

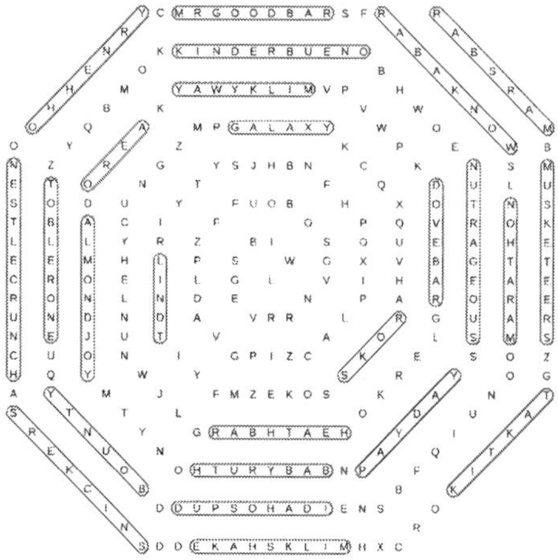

WORD LIST:

~~AERO~~
~~ALMOND JOY~~
~~BABY RUTH~~
~~BOUNTY~~
~~DOVE BAR~~
~~GALAXY~~
~~HEATH BAR~~
~~IDAHO SPUD~~
~~KINDER BUENO~~
~~KIT KAT~~
~~LINDT~~
~~MARATHON~~
~~MARS BAR~~
~~MILK SHAKE~~
~~MILKY WAY~~
~~MR GOODBAR~~
~~MUSKETEERS~~
~~NESTLE CRUNCH~~
~~NUTRAGEOUS~~
~~OH HENRY~~
~~PAYDAY~~
~~SKOR~~
~~SNICKERS~~
~~TOBLERONE~~
~~WONKA BAR~~

I am calm

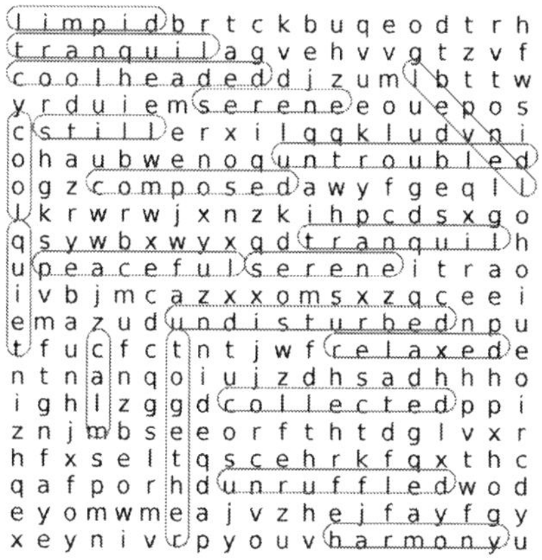

undisturbed	untroubled	coolheaded	unruffled
collected	tranquil	together	peaceful
tranquil	relaxed	serene	harmony
limpid	serene	still	level
composed	quiet	calm	cool

Dogs are number 1

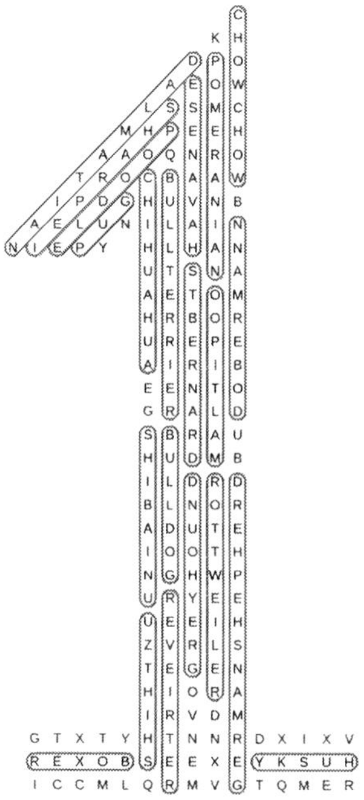

WORD LIST:

~~BOXER~~
~~BULLDOG~~
~~BULL TERRIER~~
~~CHIHUAHUA~~
~~CHOW CHOW~~
~~DALMATIAN~~
~~DOBERMANN~~
~~GERMAN SHEPHERD~~
~~GREYHOUND~~
~~HAVANESE~~
~~HUSKY~~
~~MALTIPOO~~
~~POMERANIAN~~
~~POODLE~~
~~PUG~~
~~RETRIEVER~~
~~ROTTWEILER~~
~~SHAR PEI~~
~~SHIBA INU~~
~~SHIH TZU~~
~~ST BERNARD~~

I'm happy

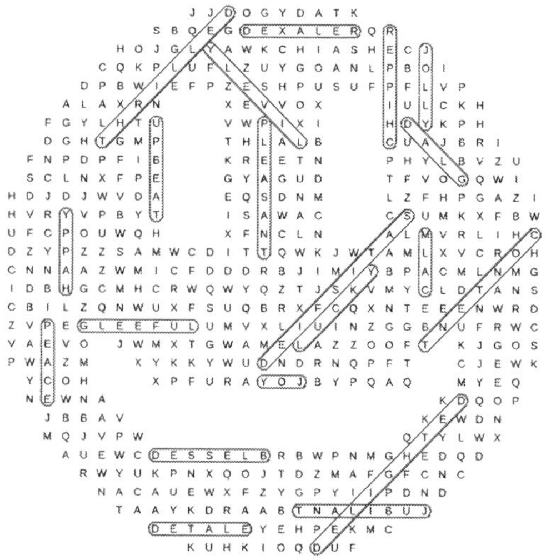

WORD LIST:

~~BLESSED~~
~~CALM~~
~~CHIPPER~~
~~CONTENT~~
~~DELIGHTED~~
~~ELATED~~
~~GLAD~~
~~GLEEFUL~~
~~HAPPY~~
~~JOLLY~~
~~JOY~~
~~JUBILANT~~
~~LIVELY~~
~~LUCKY~~
~~PEACE~~
~~PLEASANT~~
~~RELAXED~~
~~SATISFIED~~
~~THRILLED~~
~~UPBEAT~~

Birds

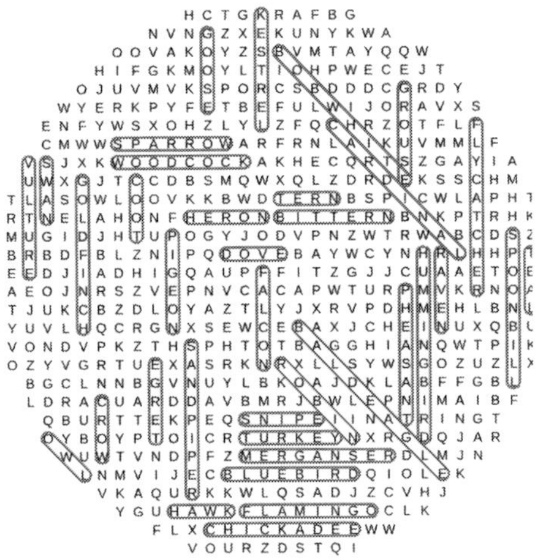

WORD LIST:

EAGLE
ERN
BIRD
VHITE
INAL
KADEE
T
V
E
EGRET
FALCON
FLAMINGO
FLYCATCHER
GOLDFINCH
GOOSE
GROUSE
HAWK
HERON
HUMMINGBIRD
KESTREL
MERGANSER
OWL
PHEASANT
PIGEON
RAVEN
ROBIN
SANDPIPER
SNIPE
SPARROV
SPOONBI
SWAN
TEAL
TERN
TURKEY
VULTURE
WOODCC

Chips

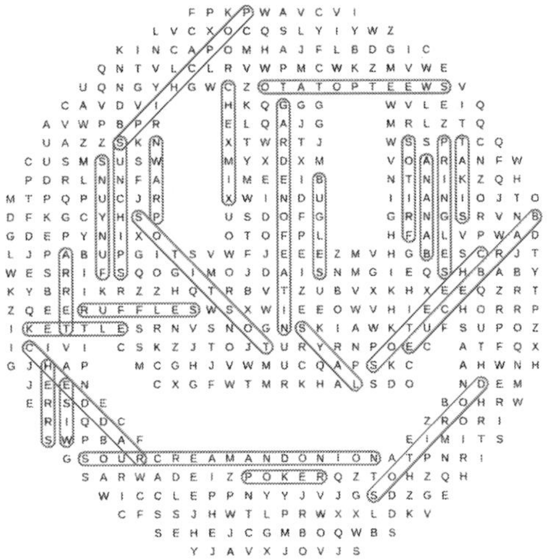

WORD LIST:

~~BANANA~~
~~BARBECUE~~
~~BUGLES~~
~~CHEDDAR~~
~~CHEETOS~~
~~CHEX MIX~~
~~DORITOS~~
~~FRITOS~~
~~FUNYUNS~~
~~GARDEN OF EATIN~~
~~HERR'S~~
~~KETTLE~~
~~LAY'S~~
~~POKER~~
~~POPCHIPS~~
~~PRAWN~~
~~PRINGLES~~
~~RUFFLES~~
~~SOUR CREAM AND ONION~~
~~SUNCHIPS~~
~~SWEET POTATO~~
~~TAKIS~~
~~TERRA~~
~~TOSTITOS~~
~~WISE~~

Inspiration

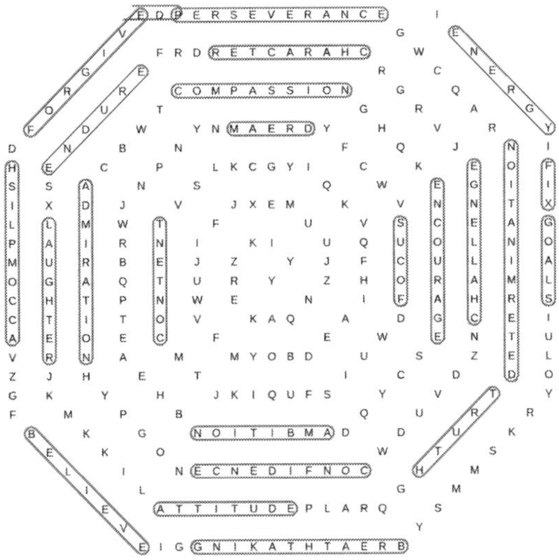

WORD LIST:

~~CCOMPLISH~~
~~DMIRATION~~
~~MBITION~~
~~TTITUDE~~
~~ELIEVE~~
~~REATHTAKING~~
~~CHALLENGE~~
~~CHARACTER~~
~~COMPASSION~~
~~CONFIDENCE~~
~~CONTENT~~
~~DETERMINATION~~
~~DREAM~~
~~ENCOURAGE~~
~~ENDURE~~
~~ENERGY~~
~~FIX~~
~~FOCUS~~
~~FORGIVE~~
~~GOALS~~
~~LAUGHTER~~
~~PERSEVERANCE~~
~~TRUTH~~

Island

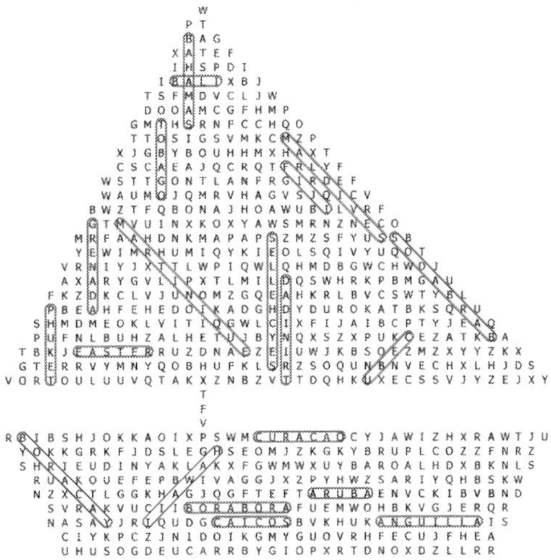

WORD LIST:

ANGUILLA
ARUBA
BAHAMAS
BALI
BARBADOS
BORABORA
BORACAY
CAICOS
CEBU
CURACAO
EASTER
FIJI
GRENADA
HAWAII
MALDIVES
MARTINIQUE
PHUKET
SEYCHELLES
TOBAGO
TRINIDAD

In sudoku every row, column, and square (9 spaces each) must be filled with numbers from 1 to 9, without duplicating a number on the same row, column, or square.

Puzzle 1

	7	6	3		8	1		2
				1		6	3	7
2			9	7			5	8
9				6	7		4	1
6		7		2				
1	4		5			7		6
8	9		7		1		6	5
7	6			3				
3		5	6		9	2	7	

Puzzle 2

8	6	5		9	7		4	
	3		8				5	7
7		2	5	6	3	1		
	2				1		7	4
		8		5	6			
3	5		7			8	6	
6		7	4		2	3		5
	8			7	5		1	
5	1		6	3		7		

Puzzle 3

6			8		7	9		
8	1			6	3			4
			2	9	1			
7		8	1				3	9
		6		7	8	4		
2	9				5	7		6
	6		3	1	2			
3	8		6				9	2
		4	7					

Puzzle 4

8		7	6		1		9	
1		6					8	2
	9		4		8		1	6
	7	3	1		2	8		5
5			3		6			7
4		2	5	8		6	3	
		8	9	1	3		6	
9	6	1						8
	2			6	5	9		1

Puzzle 5

3	8	1			7		2	4
	7		6				1	
		5	8	1			9	
	4	2		6	8	9		3
	3		9		5		6	
8		6	3				5	
	2				1	5		
6			2				8	1
7			4		6	2	3	9

Puzzle 6

5	6	7	3		2		1	
			1	6		5		
1	2					3	6	7
8		6			1	4	2	5
	7				6		9	
9	5	1	2					3
2		3	6					1
		8		1	5	2		
	1		7		3	9		4

Puzzle 7

	3	5			7	2		
	6		8				4	3
2	1		6		5		9	8
	2	8	9					
1		7				8		6
					8	1		
	8		3		2			
4	5	2		8	9		3	
		1	5			9	8	

Puzzle 8

1		4	8		7		2	
2		6	1			8	9	3
	8		2	6				
8					3		6	2
	6		7	1	2		8	
	5		4					9
		8		7	5			
5	1				8	2		6
			9	2		4		8

Puzzle 9

	5		6		2	4		
		6	4				5	2
4	2				7			
9		7	2	3			6	
1	6						2	9
	4	2		8		7		1
			5	2				7
2	3	5			4	1		
		8	1		3	2		

Puzzle 10

	4	2			8		5	
6					5		2	9
7		1	2	6				
	6	5		8	7			
3	1		5		2		8	4
2			6	4		3	7	
				5	4	9		2
1								3
5	2		9				6	

Puzzle 11

			2		7			
		4			8	7		
9	2		1	4				
4				7	2		9	
	5	9		1		3	8	
	8		9	5				7
				2	9		4	8
		6	3			5		
			7		4			

Puzzle 12

2	1					9	4	
	5							8
				2	8	3	5	7
5				1	4			
	4			9			7	
			7	3				5
3	8	2	9	7				
9							3	
	7	1					2	9

Puzzle 1

4	7	6	3	5	8	1	9	2
5	8	9	4	1	2	6	3	7
2	3	1	9	7	6	4	5	8
9	2	3	8	6	7	5	4	1
6	5	7	1	2	4	9	8	3
1	4	8	5	9	3	7	2	6
8	9	2	7	4	1	3	6	5
7	6	4	2	3	5	8	1	9
3	1	5	6	8	9	2	7	4

Puzzle 2

8	6	5	1	9	7	2	4	3
1	3	9	8	2	4	6	5	7
7	4	2	5	6	3	1	9	8
9	2	6	3	8	1	5	7	4
4	7	8	2	5	6	9	3	1
3	5	1	7	4	9	8	6	2
6	9	7	4	1	2	3	8	5
2	8	3	9	7	5	4	1	6
5	1	4	6	3	8	7	2	9

Puzzle 3

6	5	2	8	4	7	9	1	3
8	1	9	5	6	3	2	7	4
4	7	3	2	9	1	6	5	8
7	4	8	1	2	6	5	3	9
5	3	6	9	7	8	4	2	1
2	9	1	4	3	5	7	8	6
9	6	5	3	1	2	8	4	7
3	8	7	6	5	4	1	9	2
1	2	4	7	8	9	3	6	5

Puzzle 4

8	4	7	6	2	1	5	9	3
1	3	6	7	5	9	4	8	2
2	9	5	4	3	8	7	1	6
6	7	3	1	9	2	8	4	5
5	8	9	3	4	6	1	2	7
4	1	2	5	8	7	6	3	9
7	5	8	9	1	3	2	6	4
9	6	1	2	7	4	3	5	8
3	2	4	8	6	5	9	7	1

Puzzle 5

3	8	1	5	9	7	6	2	4
2	7	9	6	4	3	8	1	5
4	6	5	8	1	2	3	9	7
5	4	2	1	6	8	9	7	3
1	3	7	9	2	5	4	6	8
8	9	6	3	7	4	1	5	2
9	2	3	7	8	1	5	4	6
6	5	4	2	3	9	7	8	1
7	1	8	4	5	6	2	3	9

Puzzle 6

5	6	7	3	4	2	8	1	9
3	8	9	1	6	7	5	4	2
1	2	4	8	5	9	3	6	7
8	3	6	9	7	1	4	2	5
4	7	2	5	3	6	1	9	8
9	5	1	2	8	4	6	7	3
2	4	3	6	9	8	7	5	1
7	9	8	4	1	5	2	3	6
6	1	5	7	2	3	9	8	4

Puzzle 7

8	3	5	4	9	7	2	6	1
7	6	9	8	2	1	5	4	3
2	1	4	6	3	5	7	9	8
5	2	8	9	1	6	3	7	4
1	9	7	2	4	3	8	5	6
6	4	3	7	5	8	1	2	9
9	8	6	3	7	2	4	1	5
4	5	2	1	8	9	6	3	7
3	7	1	5	6	4	9	8	2

Puzzle 8

1	9	4	8	3	7	6	2	5
2	7	6	1	5	4	8	9	3
3	8	5	2	6	9	1	4	7
8	4	1	5	9	3	7	6	2
9	6	3	7	1	2	5	8	4
7	5	2	4	8	6	3	1	9
4	2	8	6	7	5	9	3	1
5	1	9	3	4	8	2	7	6
6	3	7	9	2	1	4	5	8

Puzzle 9

8	5	1	6	9	2	4	7	3
3	7	6	4	1	8	9	5	2
4	2	9	3	5	7	6	1	8
9	8	7	2	3	1	5	6	4
1	6	3	7	4	5	8	2	9
5	4	2	9	8	6	7	3	1
6	1	4	5	2	9	3	8	7
2	3	5	8	7	4	1	9	6
7	9	8	1	6	3	2	4	5

Puzzle 10

9	4	2	1	3	8	7	5	6
6	8	3	4	7	5	1	2	9
7	5	1	2	6	9	4	3	8
4	6	5	3	8	7	2	9	1
3	1	7	5	9	2	6	8	4
2	9	8	6	4	1	3	7	5
8	3	6	7	5	4	9	1	2
1	7	9	8	2	6	5	4	3
5	2	4	9	1	3	8	6	7

Puzzle 11

6	1	8	2	3	7	9	5	4
5	3	4	6	9	8	7	2	1
9	2	7	1	4	5	8	3	6
4	6	3	8	7	2	1	9	5
7	5	9	4	1	6	3	8	2
1	8	2	9	5	3	4	6	7
3	7	1	5	2	9	6	4	8
2	4	6	3	8	1	5	7	9
8	9	5	7	6	4	2	1	3

Puzzle 12

2	1	8	3	5	7	9	4	6
7	5	3	6	4	9	2	1	8
6	9	4	1	2	8	3	5	7
5	3	7	8	1	4	6	9	2
8	4	6	2	9	5	1	7	3
1	2	9	7	3	6	4	8	5
3	8	2	9	7	1	5	6	4
9	6	5	4	8	2	7	3	1
4	7	1	5	6	3	8	2	9

Recipes From the Inside

Homemade Peanut Brittle

2 Bags (4.5 oz. ea.) Butterscotch Discs

2 ½ Cups (12 oz.) Frosted Flakes Cereal

½ Jar of Crunchy Peanut Butter (18 oz. jar)

Step 1: Crush up the butterscotch discs into small pieces and put them in a bowl.

Step 2: Crush up the Frosted Flakes into small pieces and add to the bowl.

Step 3: Put ½ jar of peanut butter into the bowl.

Step 4: Mix everything together.

Step 5: Cook for 2 ½ minutes in the microwave and then stir.

Step 6: Cook for 1 minute more and stir again. (Repeat this step 3 more times) *it will get really hot!*

Step 7: Spread mixture onto an empty chip bag and allow to cool.

Submitted by Sam Freeman

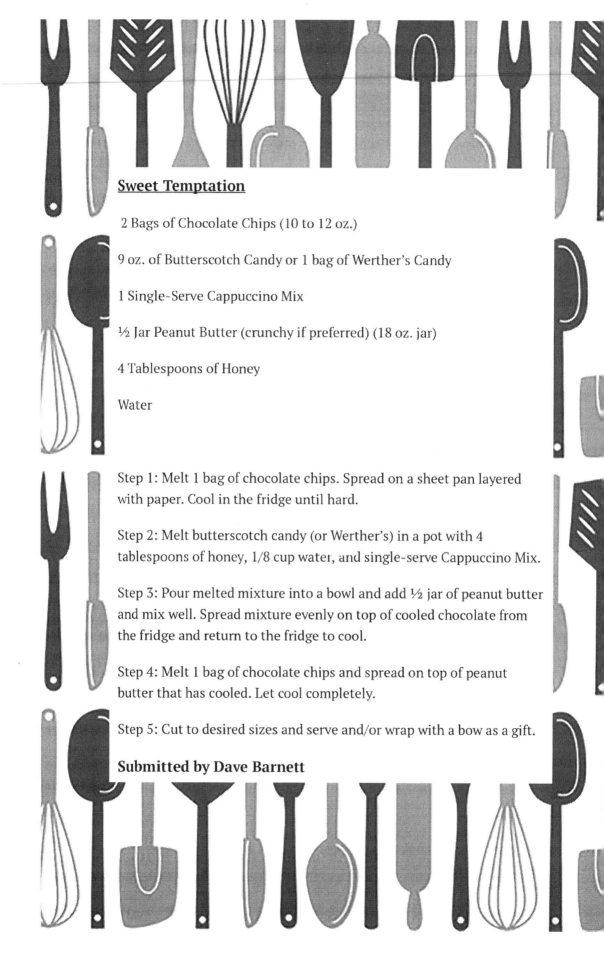

Sweet Temptation

2 Bags of Chocolate Chips (10 to 12 oz.)

9 oz. of Butterscotch Candy or 1 bag of Werther's Candy

1 Single-Serve Cappuccino Mix

½ Jar Peanut Butter (crunchy if preferred) (18 oz. jar)

4 Tablespoons of Honey

Water

Step 1: Melt 1 bag of chocolate chips. Spread on a sheet pan layered with paper. Cool in the fridge until hard.

Step 2: Melt butterscotch candy (or Werther's) in a pot with 4 tablespoons of honey, 1/8 cup water, and single-serve Cappuccino Mix.

Step 3: Pour melted mixture into a bowl and add ½ jar of peanut butter and mix well. Spread mixture evenly on top of cooled chocolate from the fridge and return to the fridge to cool.

Step 4: Melt 1 bag of chocolate chips and spread on top of peanut butter that has cooled. Let cool completely.

Step 5: Cut to desired sizes and serve and/or wrap with a bow as a gift.

Submitted by Dave Barnett

Taffy

1 bag of Coffee Creamer (8 oz.)

3 Punch Drink Packets (2.6g per packet)

Water

Step 1: Add coffee creamer to a bowl.

Step 2: Add punch drink packets to the bowl.

Step 3: Fill each empty punch drink packet with water and add to mix (3 packets of water).

Step 4: Using hands, mix well, then knead ingredients together until everything is mixed well.

Step 5: Start twisting and stretching mixture until it looks like taffy. This should take about 20 minutes.

Step 6: Spread out on wax paper and cut into strips.

Step 7: Roll strips up long ways and cut into 1" pieces and enjoy!

Submitted by Michael A. Conway

Cookie Cake

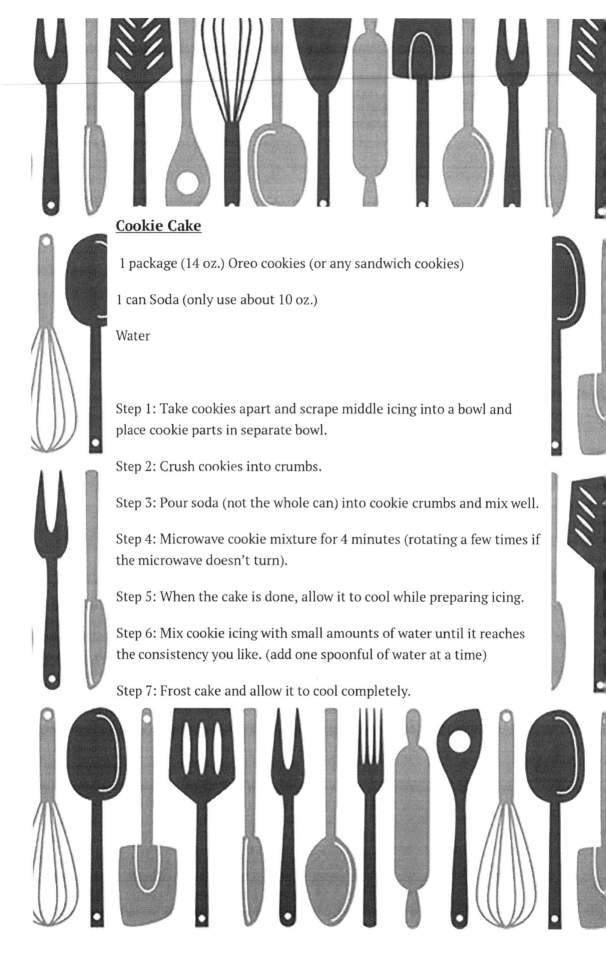

1 package (14 oz.) Oreo cookies (or any sandwich cookies)

1 can Soda (only use about 10 oz.)

Water

Step 1: Take cookies apart and scrape middle icing into a bowl and place cookie parts in separate bowl.

Step 2: Crush cookies into crumbs.

Step 3: Pour soda (not the whole can) into cookie crumbs and mix well.

Step 4: Microwave cookie mixture for 4 minutes (rotating a few times if the microwave doesn't turn).

Step 5: When the cake is done, allow it to cool while preparing icing.

Step 6: Mix cookie icing with small amounts of water until it reaches the consistency you like. (add one spoonful of water at a time)

Step 7: Frost cake and allow it to cool completely.

Quesadillas (Makes 12)

12 9" Tortilla Shells

1 bag of instant White Rice (8 oz. bag)

1 box of Banquet Chicken

5 oz. of Sausage

1 bag of Pepperoni Wheels (5 oz. bag)

16 oz. of Frozen Broccoli (thawed)

1 small block of Pepper Jack Cheese

1 small block of Cheddar Cheese

1 bottle of Squeeze Cheese

1 bottle of Ranch Dressing

Step 1: Prepare rice according to package directions and season how you like.

Step 2: Remove chicken skin and meat from bones and break into small pieces.

Step 3: Cut sausage and pepperoni into small pieces.

Step 4: Cut broccoli into small pieces.

Step 5: Cut both blocks of cheese into small pieces.

Step 6: Mix rice, chicken, sausage, pepperoni, and broccoli together in a bowl.

Step 7: Spread squeeze cheese on one side of a tortilla shell. Add some rice mixture (use about 1/12 of the mixture so you have enough for each shell). Top the rice mixture with some of both kinds of cheese.

Step 8: Put shell into microwave for 1 ½ minutes or until cheese is melted.

Step 9: Drizzle with ranch dressing.

Step 10: Fold in half and be ready to smack your lips!

Submitted by Larry Emerson

Fried Ramen Soup

1 package Ramen Soup

Sausage (or whatever meat you like)

Broccoli (or whatever veggies you like)

Water

Empty microwave popcorn bag

Step 1: Crush dry noodles into small pieces.

Step 2: Put crushed noodles with seasoning into an empty microwave popcorn bag and microwave until the noodles are browned. Check on them every 30 seconds and give them a shake.

Step 3: Add water to browned noodles and prepare according to soup directions.

Step 4: Add sausage and broccoli to soup and microwave for 1 minute.

Cheese Crust Pizza

1 12 oz. Bag of Cheese Puffs

1 11.25 oz. Bag of Chili with Beans

8 oz. Refried Beans

1 Bag Pepperoni (5 oz. bag)

1 Summer Sausage (4.5 oz.)

4 Ramen Soups (any flavor)

1 Hot or Regular Pickle

3 oz. Mozzarella Cheese

1 Bottle Squeeze Cheese

2 Single Packs of Ranch Dressing

Step 1: Crush cheese puffs and soup noodles.

Step 2: Cut up sausage, pepperoni, and pickle.

Step 3: Cut up cheese or grate with clean fly swatter.

Step 4: Boil 1 pitcher of water.

Step 5: Add a small amount of water to beans to make them easily spreadable.

Step 6: Mix crushed puffs and noodles with 1.5 pints of hot water and mush together in an empty chip bag until it forms a doughy ball. Wrap tightly in the bag and let sit for 5 minutes.

Step 7: Flatten evenly in the bag to make "pizza crust".

Step 8: Open bag and spread beans and chili over crust.

Step 9: Spread squeeze cheese on top.

Step 10: Add meat, mozzarella, and pickle.

Step 11: Drizzle with ranch dressing.

Submitted by Todd Fonville

Dots & Boxes

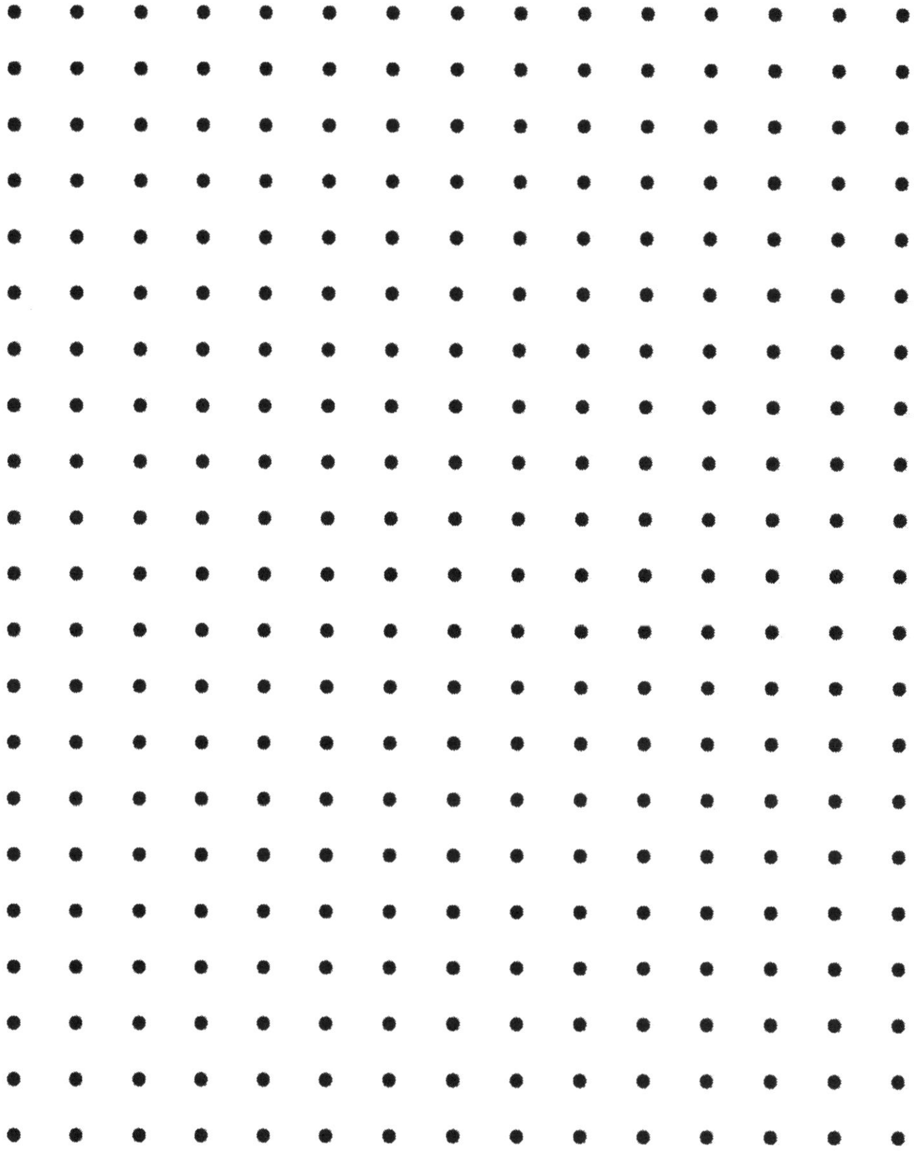

Take turns drawing horizontal or vertical lines between adjacent dots connecting them together. No diagonals!

When you complete a full square, write your initial in the box and take 1 extra turn.
If your line creates two boxes put your initial in both of them and take an extra turn.

Play continues until all the dots on the page are connected.
Count how many boxes each player has on the page.
The player with the most boxes wins!

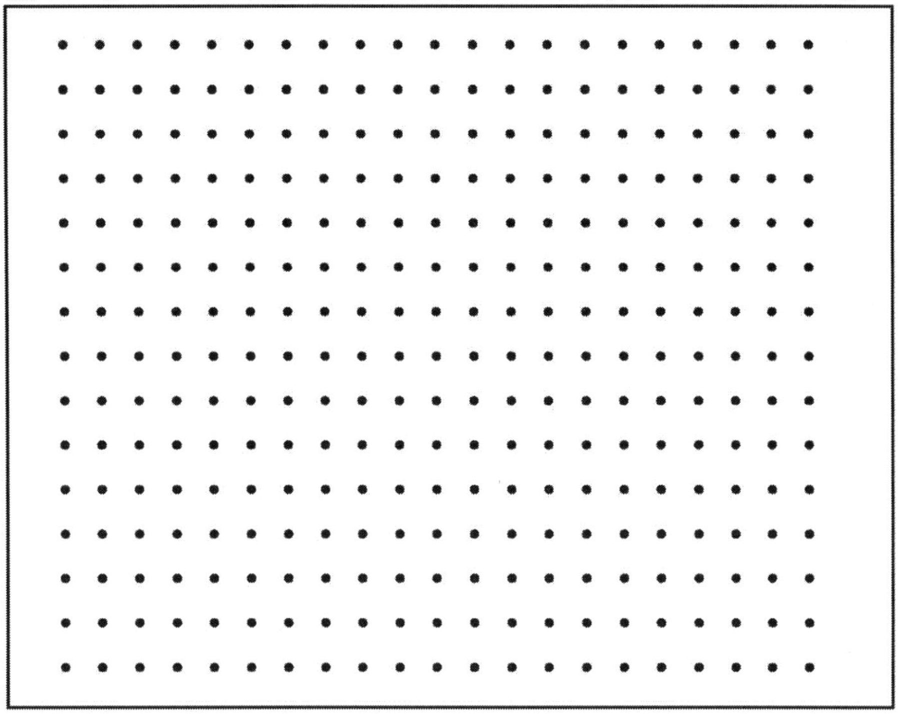

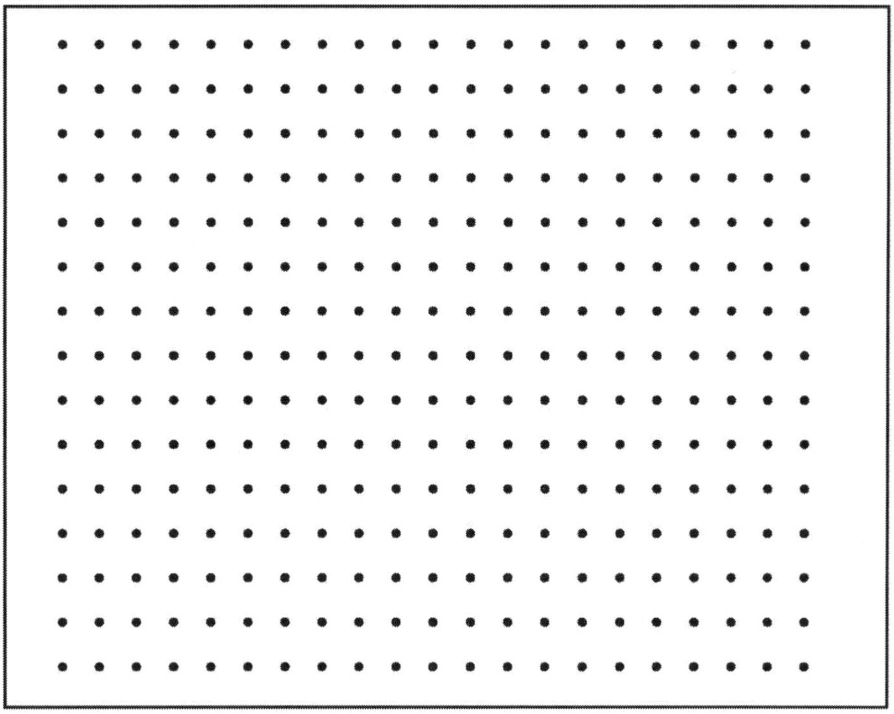

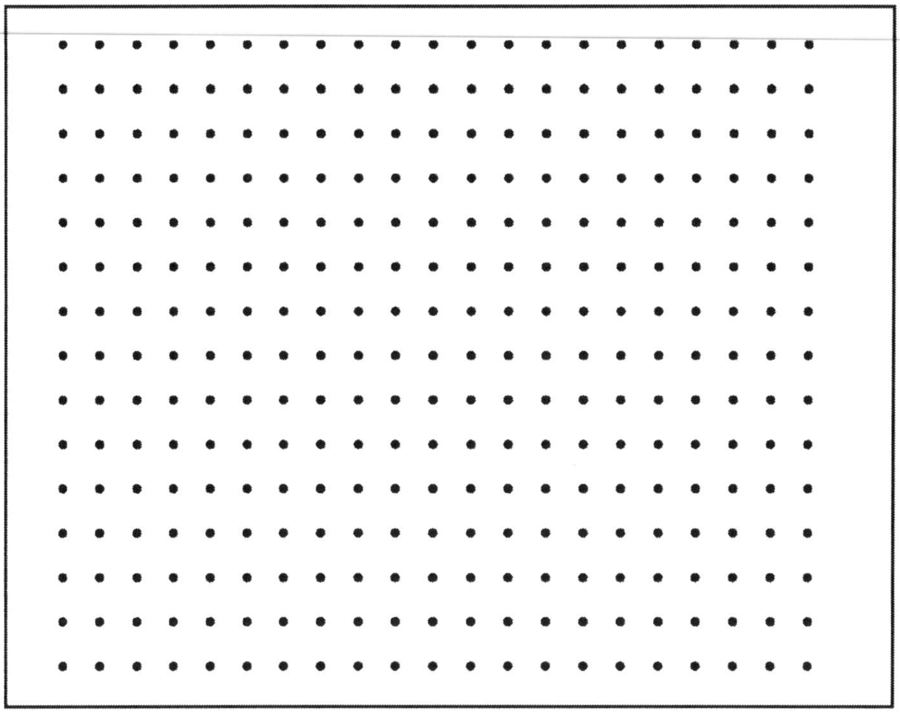

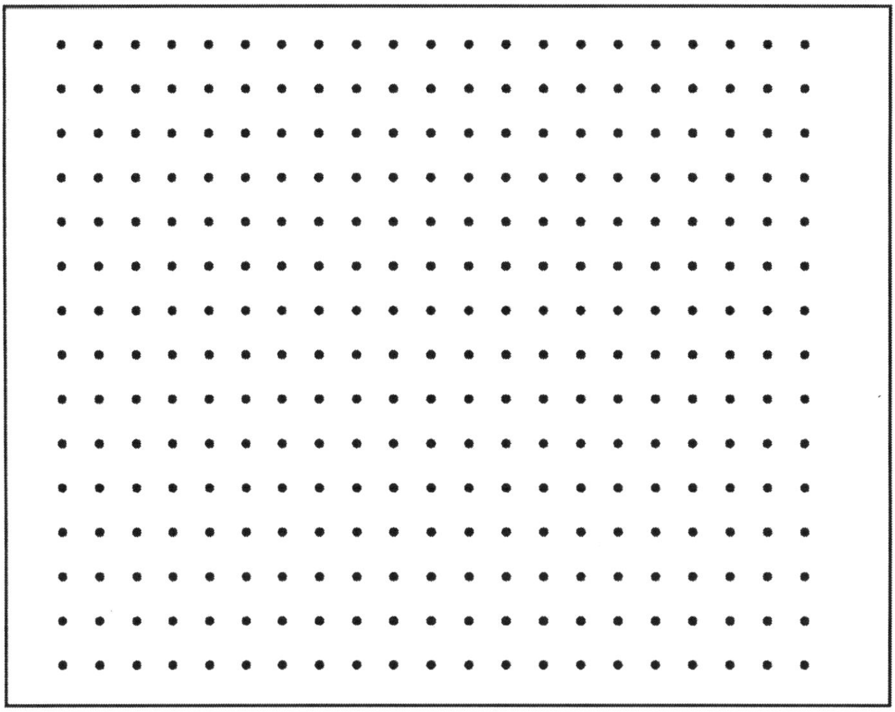

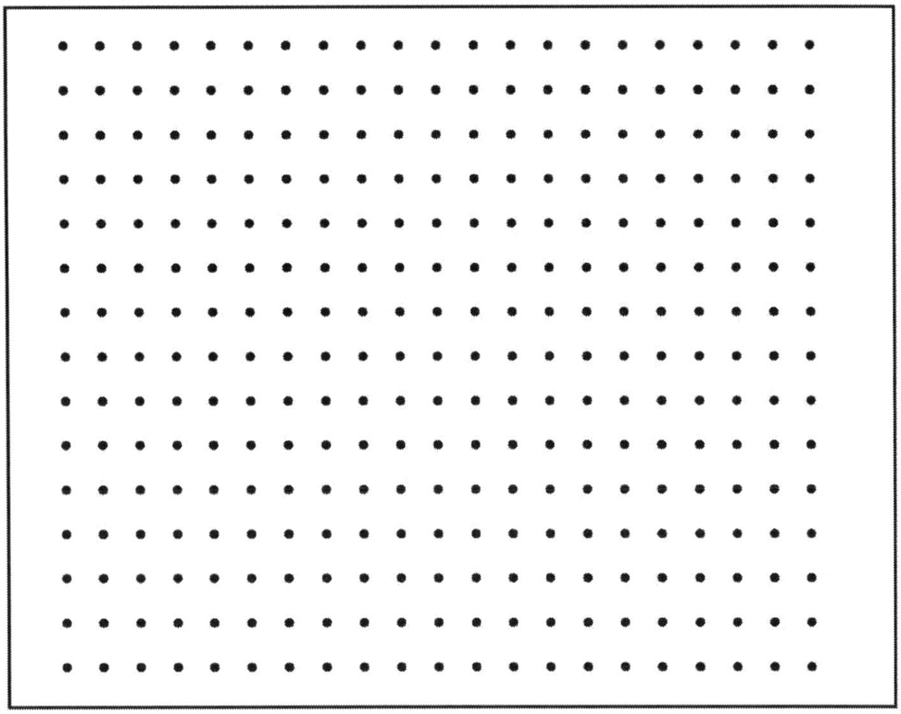

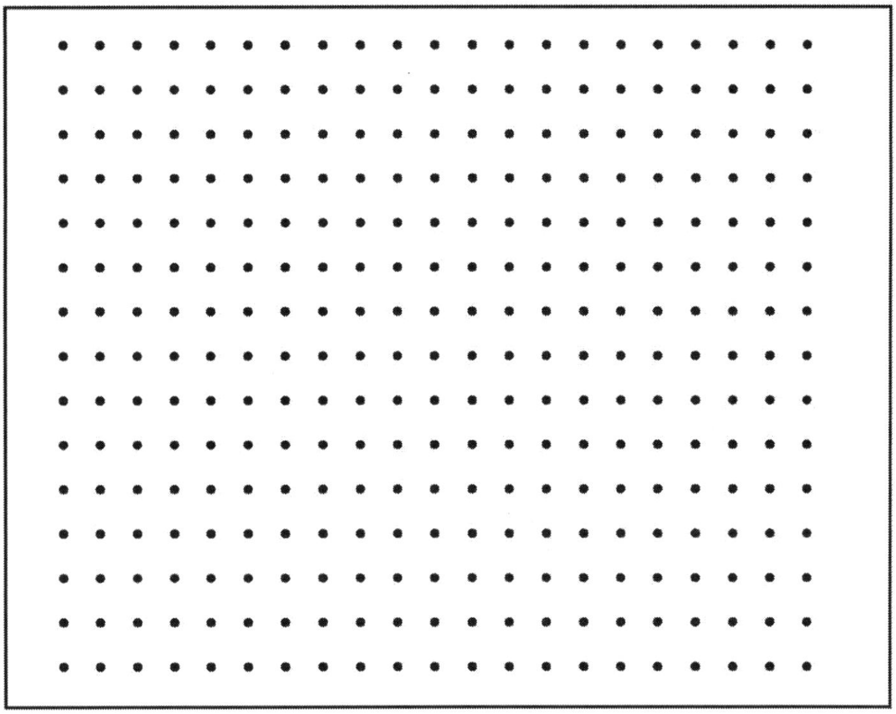

Important Dates to Remember

Important Dates to Remember

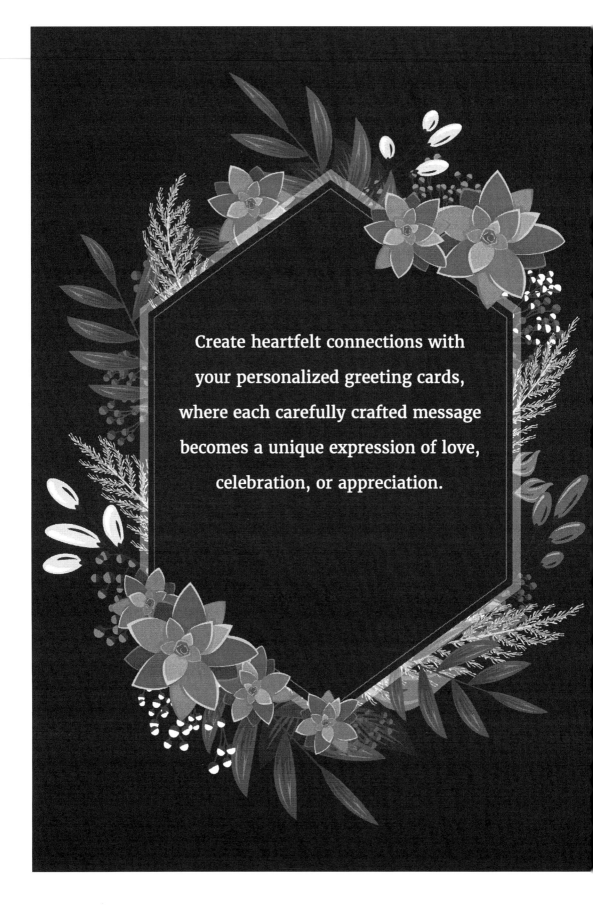

Create heartfelt connections with your personalized greeting cards, where each carefully crafted message becomes a unique expression of love, celebration, or appreciation.

Created with love by:
I Love You

All my love

Always

Created with care by:

Happy Birthay
Wishing You A Purr-Fect Day!

Created with care by:

Wishing you a speedy recovery!

Created with love
by:

Hope your
birthday is filled
with Surprises!

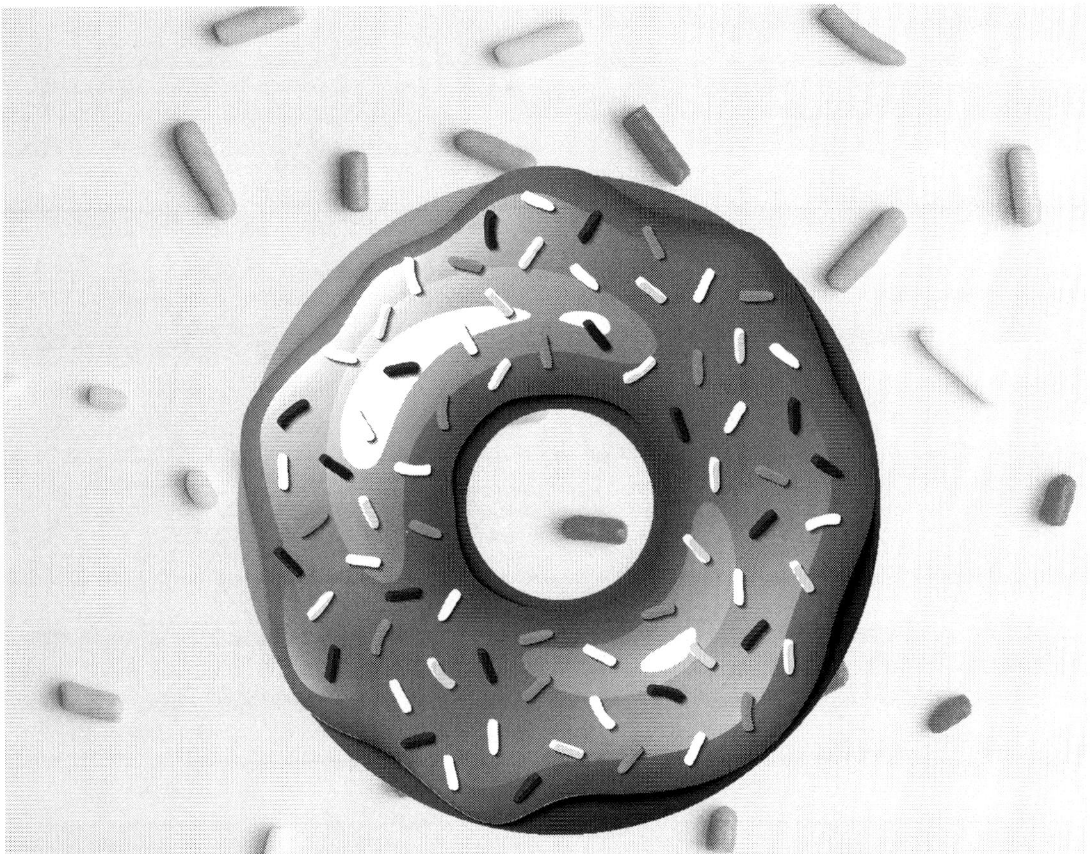

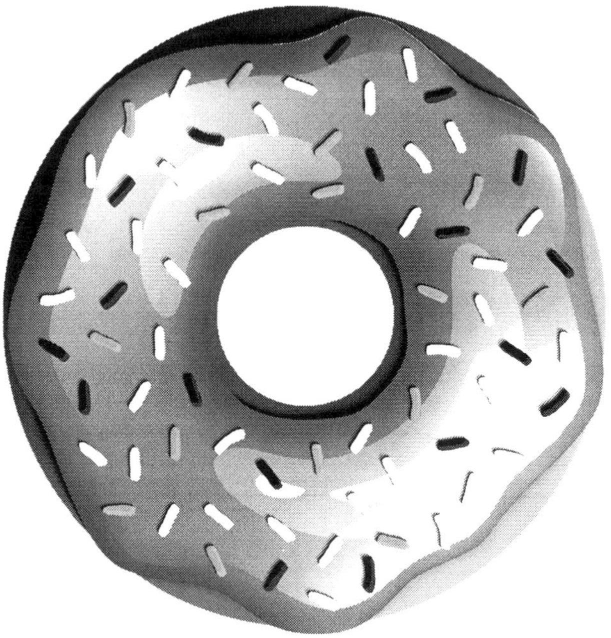

I donut know what I would do without you!

Created with love by:

Merry
EVERYTHING
&
happy
ALWAYS

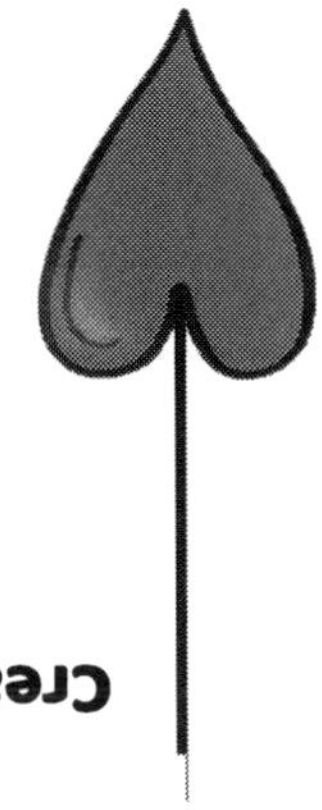

Created with care by:

Happy Valentine's Day

All My Love.
Today, Tomorrow and Always!

Created with care by:

Love you,
Mom

Created with love by:

You are
my
FAVORITE

Created with care by:

WORLD
★ GREATEST ★
DAD

LOVE
YOU
DAD

Created with care by:

Your hard work has paid off.
Here's to celebrating your success and
the bright future ahead!

Created with care by:

You are on my mind and
and in my heart!

TV Bingo

Watch TV and look for the items on your bingo card. Mark the item when you see it during the show or commercials. You can use the stars on the bottom of the page as markers or mark the corner of the square you found with a line, dot, or shape.

Announce to the group when you spot one of your squares.

A bingo is created when you have five in a row. The five in a row can be up and down, across, or diagonal.

B	I	N	G	O
money	basketball	someone laughing	book	train
diabetes ad	football	city	sports car	gum
mountain	taxi	FREE SPACE	fish	necklace
blue car	sun glasses	baby	cake	pine tree
pizza	cell phone	white car	red sweater	Mcdonald's

B	I	N	G	O
cookie	black truck	painting	airplane	taxi
candle	tooth paste	cat	lake	number 2
beard	forest	FREE SPACE	bicycle	robot
chips	plant	child	bird	bus
flag	chicken	hat	stuffed animal	tie

B	I	N	G	O
mountain	gum	red sweater	dog	white car
money	cell phone	city	sports car	cake
ice cream	book	FREE SPACE	necklace	pizza
taxi	someone laughing	wine	circle earrings	sun glasses
beer	cold medicine	baby	blue car	basketball

B	I	N	G	O
painting	tie	number 1	cookie	doctor
black truck	taxi	singing	beard	flag
flowers	wild animal	FREE SPACE	plant	candle
glasses	hat	lake	robot	tooth paste
bird	stuffed animal	chicken	cat	bus

B	I	N	G	O
diabetes ad	blue car	pine tree	Mcdonald's	sports car
cake	taxi	cell phone	mountain	palm tree
baby	gum	FREE SPACE	basketball	red dress
cold medicine	pizza	wine	city	beer
book	circle earrings	fish	money	someone laughing

B	I	N	G	O
lake	glasses	flag	tie	white car
tooth paste	chicken	taxi	chips	stuffed animal
singing	number 2	FREE SPACE	bus	painting
doctor	candle	bicycle	robot	beard
hat	candy bar	forest	airplane	number 1

B	I	N	G	O
diabetes ad	basketball	sun glasses	money	white car
beer	book	train	red dress	gum
cake	taxi	FREE SPACE	mountain	dog
fish	Mcdonald's	sports car	football	cold medicine
ice cream	red sweater	wine	cell phone	necklace

B	I	N	G	O
lake	forest	doctor	singing	hat
wild animal	cat	child	candle	taxi
glasses	bus	FREE SPACE	number 1	plant
tooth paste	stuffed animal	tie	bird	chicken
black truck	beard	bicycle	chips	painting

B	I	N	G	O
cell phone	white car	red sweater	circle earrings	train
dog	necklace	baby	sports car	cold medicine
diabetes ad	book	FREE SPACE	blue car	ice cream
money	fish	wine	someone laughing	cake
pizza	gum	casino	palm tree	taxi

B	I	N	G	O
hat	bicycle	stuffed animal	cookie	white car
bus	flowers	taxi	child	lake
flag	forest	FREE SPACE	tooth paste	black truck
number 1	tie	beard	candle	painting
plant	cat	singing	robot	airplane

Thanks

Sam Freeman, Dave Barnett, Michael A. Conway, Todd Fonville, and Larry Emerson for contributing recipes. Special thanks to Mr. Emerson for compiling the recipes.

To our readers,

If you've received this inmate activity book as a gift, we encourage you to discuss it with the person who gave it to you. Share your thoughts on the activities, their impact on your well-being, and how they've helped you pass the time. Discuss the aspects of the book that have been most beneficial. Your words can inspire and guide others seeking constructive outlets during incarceration.

Please, please, please ask your loved ones to leave honest reviews on Amazon or Barnes & Noble. These reviews provide valuable feedback for us and help potential readers make informed decisions about the book's impact on their loved ones.

We deeply appreciate your support in our inmate activity book community. Your feedback is invaluable, and we eagerly await your reviews. Thank you for your time, and may this book continue to be a source of inspiration and growth during your incarceration.

Kindest regards - Beth and Patricia

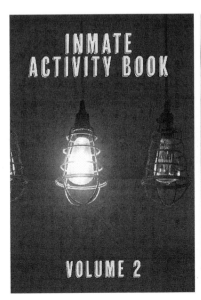

Made in the USA
Las Vegas, NV
18 November 2024

12078708R00083